DECOLONIZING EDUCATIONAL RESEARCH

Decolonizing Educational Research examines the ways through which coloniality manifests in contexts of knowledge and meaning making, specifically within educational research and formal schooling. Purposefully situated beyond popular deconstructionist theory and anthropocentric perspectives, the book investigates the long-standing traditions of oppression, racism, and white supremacy that are systemically reseated and reinforced through societal institutions. Through these meaningful explorations into the unfixed and often interrupted narratives of culture, history, place, and identity, a bold, timely, and hopeful vision emerges to conceive of how research in secondary and higher education institutions might break free of colonial genealogies and their widespread complicities.

Leigh Patel is Associate Professor of Education in the Department of Teacher Education/Special Education, Curriculum and Instruction at the Lynch School of Education, Boston College, USA.

Series in Critical Narrative
Donaldo Macedo, Series Editor
University of Massachusetts Boston

Now in Print

The Hegemony of English
by Donaldo Macedo, Bessie Dendrinos, and Panayota Gounari (2003)

Letters from Lexington: Reflections on Propaganda
New Updated Edition
by Noam Chomsky (2004)

Pedagogy of Indignation
by Paulo Freire (2004)

Howard Zinn on Democratic Education
by Howard Zinn, with Donaldo Macedo (2005)

How Children Learn: Getting Beyond the Deficit Myth
by Terese Fayden (2005)

The Globalization of Racism
edited by Donaldo Macedo and Panayota Gounari (2006)

Daring to Dream: Toward a Pedagogy of the Unfinished
by Paulo Freire (2007)

Class in Culture
by Teresa L. Ebert and Mas'ud Zavarzadeh (2008)

Dear Paulo: Letters from Those Who Dare Teach
by Sonia Nieto (2008)

Uncommon Sense from the Writings of Howard Zinn (2008) Paulo Freire and the Curriculum
by Georgios Grollios (2009)

Freedom at Work: Language, Professional, and Intellectual Development in Schools
by Maria E. Torres-Guzman with Ruth Swinney (2009)

The Latinization of U.S. Schools: Successful Teaching and Learning in Shifting Cultural Contexts
by Jason G. Irizarry (2011)

Culture and Power in the Classroom: Educational Foundations for the Schooling of Bicultural Students
by Antonia Darder (2011)

Changing Lives: Working with Literature in an Alternative Sentencing Program
by Taylor Stoehr (2013)

Seeds of Freedom: Liberating Education in Guatemala
by Clark Taylor (2013)

Pedagogy of Commitment
by Paulo Freire (2014)

Latino Civil Rights in Education: La Lucha Sigue
edited by Anaida Colón-Muñiz and Magaly Lavadenz (2016)

Decolonizing Educational Research: From Ownership to Answerability
by Lisa Patel (2016)

DECOLONIZING EDUCATIONAL RESEARCH

From Ownership to Answerability

Leigh Patel

Routledge
Taylor & Francis Group

NEW YORK AND LONDON

First published 2016
by Routledge
711 Third Avenue, New York, NY 10017

and by Routledge
2 Park Square, Milton Park, Abingdon, Oxon OX14 4RN

Routledge is an imprint of the Taylor & Francis Group, an informa business

© 2016 Taylor & Francis

Library of Congress Cataloging in Publication Data
Names: Patel, Leigh.
Title: Decolonizing educational research : from ownership to answerability / Leigh Patel.
Description: New York : Routledge, 2015. | Series: Series in critical narrative | Includes bibliographical references and index.
Identifiers: LCCN 2015025506| ISBN 9781138998711 (hardback) | ISBN 9781138998728 (pbk.) | ISBN 9781315658551 (ebook)
Subjects: LCSH: Minorities--Education (Higher)--United States. | Dissertations, Academic--United States.
Classification: LCC LC3731 .P37 2015 DDC 378.1/982--dc23
LC record available at http://lccn.loc.gov/2015025506

ISBN: 978-1-138-99871-1 (hbk)
ISBN: 978-1-138-99872-8 (pbk)
ISBN: 978-1-315-65855-1 (ebk)

Typeset in Bembo
by Saxon Graphics Ltd, Derby

Printed and bound in the United States of America by Publishers Graphics, LLC on sustainably sourced paper.

Dedication

This book is dedicated to my mother, Sharda Patel.
Thank you for teaching us how to love and trust ourselves, against odds.
Every joy and accomplishment we experience is because of you.

CONTENTS

ACKNOWLEDGMENTS

For a milestone birthday, I asked all of the people in my life to forego presents and, instead, to handwrite one thing they were absolutely sure of from their experiences in this world. I believe that one of the very things of which I am absolutely certain is that we accomplish nothing completely individually. What follows here, then, is my best, albeit undoubtedly partial, recognition of the many people and communities that have supported me to be better able to do this work. They are all my teachers.

First and foremost, I must thank the forced migrant and Indigenous communities in Hawai'i, Turtle Island, and Australia for welcoming me and teaching me how to understand their and my trajectories relative to each other. Fifteen years ago, I would have never foreseen writing this book, but that is truly when the impetus for this thinking began. It was in concert with members of those communities that I first began to understand, implicitly and then more explicitly, the always interrelated but never equivalent locations we have, and our duties therein. It was also in conversation with, sometimes in close proximity and sometimes through distal readings, that I refined the ideas presented here. Many people took an interest in the topic and led me to the readings that have been foundational to this bounded version. Specifically, I'd like to thank Malia Villegas, Eve Tuck, Aileen Moreton-Robinson, Allan Luke, Linda Tuhiwai Smith, Michelle Fine, Kathy Au, Val Tsuchiya, Avis Masuda, and Anna Sumida. All of these scholars have strengthened my understanding of the core roots and purposes of coloniality.

I'd also like to acknowledge the dozens of doctoral students over the years who have been conversant with me in research methods courses as we strained against the pervasive lie that there can be any knowledge or pursuit of knowledge devoid of context, power, and material impact. Such conversations require going directly against the grain of the much more ubiquitous themes of neutrality, objectivity, and best practices. I thank the many students who diverted from graduate study as career preparation to engage with research as ethically and morally bound endeavors. Specifically, I'd like to thank Alex Gurn and Nick Drane for being conversants with me through early and later drafts of this work.

Writing itself is always a necessary and simultaneously arduous practice for me. I would never get far but for the fantastically knowledgeable and responsive readers, editors, and companion writers in my life. Editors Dean Birkenkamp, Catherine Bernard, and Daniel Schwartz provided plenty of encouragement, always needed, as well as smart, pointed reads of the work. Thank you to Donaldo Macedo for his early and consistent support of this work. And gratitude to my writing partner for years, Wayne Rhodes, who read draft upon draft upon draft.

Finally, and most importantly, I offer recognition and love to the people who keep me going. From intellectual engagement to companionship, and those often mixed together, you are the loved ones in my life who love me back in such ways that make me better. Much love to Nita, Prakash, Susan, and Gabriela.

FOREWORD

Eve Tuck

Before you is a gorgeous, unsettling, and satisfying book. In this foreword, I am the fortunate one who gets to celebrate the publication of *Decolonizing Educational Research: From Ownership to Answerability*; I also get to anticipate the rippling actions this book will inspire in our field(s). I have been waiting for this book to come out for a long time – the wait has been part of Patel's approach to writing *Decolonizing Educational Research*, as she describes in her introduction. Still, I feel that I have been waiting for a book like this for much longer than Patel's path to writing it; perhaps I feel that our field has always been waiting for a book like this.

If we pay attention to Patel, we can take up what she has offered as a pedagogy of pausing (my words, not hers) which involves intentionally engaging in suspension of one's own premises and projects, but always with a sense of futurity. Pausing is an insertion of *space* in time. In her introduction, Patel describes the deep pauses that fomented this book as useful, necessary, productive interruptions and as opportunities to quiet down to see what can be learned. Pausing unsettles the relentless march of educational research toward production—of data, publications, problems, gaps, communities, schools, and futures. In Chapter 5, Patel writes that the best move that educational researchers can do is to "pause in order to reach beyond" the typical tropes of our field.

In pausing, Patel urges us toward plain stopping some of the worst habits of our field. Among those bad habits are the ways that educational researchers have shied away from naming and condemning white supremacy, racism, and anti-blackness through deployment of racial proxies, designed to signal race without meaningfully or materially attending to its workings. In Chapter 2, after providing an alternate way to understand function and dysfunction, Patel describes educational research as a dysfunctional space, operating far afield from its commonly stated intentions. In one of my favorite treatises on "disFUNKtion,"

Robin D.G. Kelley (1997) explains how the myth that racism has been removed from U.S. society persists, despite the evidence of continued attacks on Black and urban life. Part of the dysfunction of this persistent myth – similar to the dysfunction that Patel attributes to educational research – has to do with widespread zealousness in blaming problems on children and families, not the policies and corporate interests which drive dispossession. Kelley notes, "Whatever the narrative and whoever the source, these cultural and ideological constructions of ghetto life have irrevocably shaped public policy, scholarship, and social movements" (1997, p. 9).

Patel locates the most concern in the tendency for educational research to invest in and recenter settler colonialism. Patel states this clearly in the Introduction,

> As a critical scholar, I contend that this busyness around claiming and refusing identity markers has oftentimes led to critical scholarship doing more work that ultimately recenters colonial projects of categorizing rather than generating spaces beyond.
>
> (p. 3)

She notes that settler colonialism "trains people to see each other, the land, and knowledge as property, to be in constant insatiable competition for limited resources" (Chapter 4, p. 72). This is the point of departure offered in this book, from other critiques of educational research practices, and other descriptions of social justice in education. In settler colonialism, accumulation of (Indigenous) land (turned property) is the most salient goal. Further, settler colonialism seeks to turn Indigenous land into property and regards Black life as fungible (see King, 2014). As Indigenous writer Leanne Simpson observes,

> Black and Indigenous communities of struggle are deeply connected through our experiences with colonialism, oppression, and white supremacy. Indigenous and Black people are disproportionately attacked and targeted by the state, and, in fact, policing in Turtle Island was born of the need to suppress and oppress Black and Indigenous resistance to colonialism and slavery.
>
> (2014, n.p.)

Indeed, securing of private property and maintenance of private property are the major preoccupations of settler occupation. Security and suppression are entwined in the dispossession of Indigenous and Black communities.

Patel observes that all others in settler colonial structures are positioned to strive toward but never achieve settler status (and settler property). Social science research, specifically educational research, is part of this accumulation by (Indigenous) dispossession. Thus, Patel puts into effect an important crossroads for critical educational research: either continue to rely upon and refuel coloniality, or work toward its undoing. In that undoing, Patel urges readers toward several aims in Chapter 1, including recognizing: 1) the ways that coloniality is manifested in both meaning and materiality in educational research; 2) the role that educational research performs in "perpetuating and refreshing" colonial relationships among people, practices, and land; and 3) the link between differences in educational outcomes and (ongoing) colonization. Patel speaks to the ways in which ongoing settler colonialism and related forms of oppression are tolerated in nation-states which purport to value equality and freedom. Patel attends to the so-called achievement gap as an extended example of the choices available to educational researchers. She questions how the gap has functioned (and dysfunctioned) to cover over and perpetuate legacies of colonization.

Perhaps the most important move that *Decolonizing Educational Research* makes is from ownership to answerability. This intervention on the conditions and terms of our efforts is among the most inspiring shifts that I have encountered in our field. In Chapter 4, Patel notes,

> Considering educational research's role in the perpetuation of settler–slave–Indigenous relationships, those of us employed as educational researchers are answerable to these deep trajectories. Given these deep trajectories, research and researchers who have succeeded have been validated through settler colonial structures of schooling and consequentially are answerable, minimally, to working to dismantle those structures.
>
> (p. 74)

The implications of a move from ownership to answerability are substantial, prompting an altogether different pivot point for what counts and what is excellent in educational research. In emphasizing answerability, Patel is emphasizing relationships, interactions, echoes, and connections – she is emphasizing complexity, enfoldings, multiplicities, and contingencies. I sincerely hope that this is just one of the contributions that our field will take up from this volume.

Decolonizing Educational Research asks big questions about the legacies of settler colonialism in educational research, settler justifications for research, the obligations of profiteering, reluctant, and forced settlers to dismantle settler colonialism, and futurities outside of these legacies. Patel observes her own pausing on or between the terms anticolonial and decolonial – noting it is not a sequential pause, not a temporal ordering – but a reflection on the significance of land and materiality in defining decolonization. This pausing is not reconciled in this volume, but it is also not haphazardly, or too quickly, or too conveniently discarded. What is clear even in the pause, as Patel observes in Chapter 5, is the insufficiency of concepts such as "inclusion" and "equity" to confront the erasure and dehumanization of settler colonialism.

What I appreciate most about Patel's approach is her refusal of the notion of the inevitable. Though deeply invested in settler colonialism, educational research is not too forgone to be reconfigured. She describes this, her "optimist offering," most concretely in Chapter 3, refusing to "concede that the pursuit of knowledge is doomed to colonial referents" (p. 48). While marking that there is much difficult work to do, there are no ways around it, especially for those of us who love the labors of learning.

In *Decolonizing Educational Research* Patel provides a praxis of pausing and even a way to listen for the balk as a sound of learning. She calls for educational research to be answerable to Indigenous people, answerable to colonized peoples on Indigenous land, and answerable to Black people on Indigenous land. Many authors try to write a timeless tome, something to sit on the shelf for many generations. Other authors try to write the definitive volume on a subject, so that the book may be closed on a topic. Both impulses come from a closed logic of universality and finality. Instead, Patel writes right into the most timely and vexing contradictions of educational research. Her optimism throbs at so many pulse points; optimism for the conversation to shift meaningfully, for a proliferation of works on decolonizing educational research. For these reasons, Patel has done something quite generous and generative for educational research: she has offered it an opportunity to reframe and redirect itself. She has offered it a lifeline.

References

Kelley, R.D.G. (1997). *Yo'mama's disfunktional!: Fighting the Culture Wars in Urban America.* Boston, MA: Beacon Press.

King, T.L. (2014, June 10). Labor's Aphasia: Toward Antiblackness as Constitutive to Settler Colonialism. [Blog post] *Decolonization: Indigeneity, Education & Society.* Last accessed July 31, 2015 at https://decolonization.wordpress.com/2014/06/10/labors-aphasia-toward-antiblackness-as-constitutive-to-settler-colonialism.

Simpson, L.B. (2014, November 28). Indict the System: Indigenous and Black Connected Resistance. [Blog post] *Leanne Betasamosake Simpson.* Last accessed July 31, 2015 at http://leannesimpson.ca/indict-the-system-indigenous-black-connected-resistance.

INTRODUCTION

A few years ago, I outlined the scope and sequence of this book. Contract in hand, I set about delivering on my end of the agreement. However, each time I drafted portions of the book, I experienced deep pauses that held the corpus of the work at bay. In the constant march of time as understood through Western colonizing frameworks, this is bad. Those pauses meant missing deadlines, and that may have meant that someone elsewhere was writing while I was not. Also bad. But pausing is useful, even necessary, particularly in these modern times in which colonial projects have shaped technology, knowledge, and connection to be a veritable nonstop stimulation of tweets, status updates, and deadlines, all competing for our attention. And, in turn, we compete for each other's attention (Lanham, 2007). Pausing, though, can be a productive interruption to these competitive ways of being, doing, and knowing, and they also hold potential learning within them (Shahjahan, 2014). In fact, in hindsight, I view the pauses I had as entirely required to best write and perhaps more effectively read this book.

The first pause I felt was about the practical and generative utility of a deconstructive analysis of educational research, in essence a wondering about the limits of critique. As has been long documented about critical analyses of society and knowledge production, they can result in nihilism among the deconstructed shards (Lather, 1986). Put another way, once tools of societal analysis are learned and used, including the well-worn social categories of race, class, gender, and ability, there is very little that cannot be deconstructed.

Deconstruction for deconstruction's sake has also, in some instances, become a *fait accompli* venture that ironically allows for little engagement, historicity, connection to purpose, and theories of change (Tuck, 2009). Theories of change, as Tuck explains, are often missing from even the most robust critiques of societal structures. Left unarticulated, there often seems to be a tacit theory of change that through critique, through the articulation of wrong or malignancy in society, that transformation will occur. However, calling attention to something does not automatically mean its transformation.

For example, recent years have witnessed social media takedowns of various ill-advised and often oppressive comments from famous and not so famous people who become infamous through the social media takedown. The effects have been many, including a lurching effect from each week's public display of racist/ sexist/classist/sometimes ableist comments and ensuing outcry. These repetitive outcries do not, however, necessarily build cumulative analysis of the difference between, say a racially biased text and a racist one, not to mention the pervasiveness of systemic racism. To this point, a popular press book (Ronson, 2015) explores the nature of public shaming via social media but equivocates across the historical, cultural, and political structures in which a range of emotions, including shame, are experienced. One pointed example which acts as an anchor for the book, is the case of a white female public relations executive whose professional life was thrown off-track for a year, after a racist tweet she sent before flying to Africa from North America went viral through social media. The tweet was racist both because of the bigoted content and because of systemic power the PR rep held as a white, upper middle class professional woman. Evidenced through both the temporary disruption to her professional life and the positioning of this case as the empathetic center in a book addressing public shaming, longer standing patterns of coloniality and oppression can be easily invisibilized and reseated even amidst discussion of social interactions. In other words, while social media attention to racist comments can be a way of raising awareness, when material structures are not addressed centrally, they stay intact, reseating problematic uneven understandings of systemic, long-standing forms of oppression.

The role of critical analysis and deconstruction of words is a particularly confounding issue in this contemporary context of racism without racists. Because overtly racist words and legal codes are perceived to have been expunged (Bonilla-Silva, 2009) and shunned, but coloniality and segmentation of humans is no less vital to many stratified societies, various forms of racial proxies (Perry, 2011) have come into existence to do the work of racially sorting without uttering the words "race" or "white supremacy." In this context, then, the colonial, racist, and otherly oppressive impact of words and deeds cannot be modernistically understood, with single meanings held constant regardless of context. Shame, to draw from the example above, is never disconnected from cultural histories and presence of inequity and oppression. While meaning as a function of context has been a mainstay premise of postmodern thought, the grip of modernist-leaning claims (so and so said something racist) can ironically and unproductively obscure the pervasiveness of coloniality. The location of some actions as within and others outside of systemic coloniality mutes and collapses necessary conversations, not only about the function and impact of oppressive deeds and acts but also about the theories of change for more desired dynamics.

The kinds of critiques that erupt in the media over various performances of oppression are, in many ways, a sign that tools of deconstruction have some utility, but in their disconnect from theorizing more generative spaces and how we might arrive there, these same tools of deconstruction show their limits.

Relative to the potential, promise, and need to interrupt coloniality, there are conceptual limits to deconstructive analyses, particularly considering that many of the most popular deconstructionist theories (e.g., Marxism) work from an anthropocentric stance, which compromises their abilities to reach far enough into the contours, functions, and imperative of coloniality. While there are wide and important differences between epistemic traditions, the beginning, middle, and end of such critiques typically assume a center of humans and how they interact with each other, often around issues of identity, with land and place as a backdrop (Tuck and McKenzie, 2015). As a critical scholar, I contend that this busyness around claiming and refusing identity markers has oftentimes led to critical scholarship doing more work that ultimately recenters colonial projects of categorizing rather than generating spaces beyond. Critique is necessary for noting the contours of colonial logics but it is insufficient for imagining into existence praxes that decolonize

In her book, *Red Pedagogy*, Sandy Grande (2004) guides the reader to understand the ways in which critical theorizations of identity and subjectivity fall short of reckoning with the needs of Indigenous peoples living in coloniality. She articulates how identity is trapped by an essentialism; and subjectivity, while offering a hybrid freeing from essentialism, fails to contend directly with the material consequences of how identities are necessarily essentially ascribed by a settler state. Neither, then, can adequately speak to the needs of Indigenous peoples and their relations to a colonizing state formed to evacuate Indigenous peoples themselves from land. Coloniality is imbued throughout the language of identity politics. As Grande puts it, to tease out and

> assign primary to certain aspects of Indian-ness as "the definition" would not only grossly oversimplify the complexity of American Indian subjectivity (forcing what is fundamentally traditional, spatial, and interconnected into the modern, temporal, and epistemic frames of Western theory), but also reenact objectification of Indians set in motion by the Dawes commission over a century ago.
>
> (p. 98)

Grande's work in *Red Pedagogy* provides content through a format that engages in critique and generative thought beyond what critique alone can offer, particularly Marxist and Marxist-derived criticism. She maintains a consistent integrity to what Indigenous theories of self-determination, education, and survivance afford and why they are so crucial to wrest living beings from the grip of coloniality. Reading Grande's work, along with extant critical Indigenous scholarship that has addressed decolonization, including work by, but certainly not limited to, Linda Tuhiwai Smith, Eve Tuck, Marie Battiste, Bryan McKinley Brayboy, Audra Simpson, and Shawn Wilson figured in my second substantive pause: who am I, a nonNative person, to write this book?

Critiques of coloniality are by no means the sole domain of Indigenous scholars. Classic works by Gloria Anzaldúa, Aime Cesaire, Chela Sandoval, Gayatri Spivak, Sylvia Wynter, Hortense Spillers, Trinh T. Minh-ha, Frantz Fanon, Donaldo Macedo, and bell hooks, among many others, have all adroitly addressed the origins, contours, and impacts of coloniality. However, there has been a surge recently in the use of the terms and stances of decolonization, occupation, and sovereignty, with varying and often problematic historical understanding of coloniality. As one particularly notable example, the Occupy Wall Street movement that began in September of 2011 used this language of occupying as a way of speaking back to the wealthiest land owning class in the United States. Muted until critiqued, though, was the historical and contemporary fact that New York City, the home of the Occupy movement, is itself located on the traditional lands of the Algonquin people and has been occupied since the first breath of European invasion. As Anishaabe environmental activist Robert Desjarlait noted, "The question is – the decolonization of what, or whom? How can decolonization be a part of the process if the occupiers are occupying land?" (2011, para. 9). While these questions can and should be raised by Indigenous and nonIndigenous peoples alike, the recent increase in uses of the term, "decolonize," has prompted consideration of the material effects when the term is used loosely. In their timely and thorough article, "Decolonization is not a metaphor," Eve Tuck and K. Wayne Yang (2012) provide thoughtful analysis on the ways that, when used metaphorically and imprecisely, decolonization serves to further erase Indigeneity and reseat white settler privilege.

The third location of a significant pause I experienced was whether educational research could, in fact, become something other than colonizing, whether an entity borne of and beholden to coloniality could somehow wrest itself free of this genealogy. Having been an educator in secondary and tertiary institutional settings, I have often felt that my love of learning and knowledge as uncontainable has led me to be in a constant state of heartbreak, since formal schooling has so little to do with either. Since its inception in the United States, versus the pre-existing practices of Native peoples, formal schooling has had far more to do with the project of coloniality than it has with learning, teaching, or co-existence. This is not to say that learning and human growth doesn't happen frequently within schooling settings, but it is often the result of individuals who have committed themselves to swimming upstream, circumventing the design of schools as sites of discipline and social reproduction, and created spaces beyond hegemonic policies and practices.

While my initial pause about the possibility of decolonizing educational research remains, it is more specific. I am, to put it mildly, dubious about the likelihood of the academy, in its current cultural structure, embracing any goal that isn't about social reproduction and re-inscribing preferred knowledge. At least not in the foreseeable immediate future. However, research and learning have a far longer and richer history and reach than higher education as colonial enterprise. My more specific pause, then, is about how educational research, within and likely moreso beyond the academy, can take on the work of recalibration. How can it rethink itself to be answerable to learning, knowledge, and living beings' needs? As I explore further in Chapter 3, to counter coloniality in educational research means that we must disambiguate schooling from learning (Battiste, 2013; Patel, 2013), to foreground questions of what and whom to be answerable to.

Across these pauses, my duty has been to quiet down enough so that I can learn from and within those unsettled pauses, particularly related to the ways that educational research should pause far more frequently in its seemingly unrelenting quest for data and publications. I open this book with these pauses as a possible example of the sort of rupture and change to being and learning that may be appropriate to counter the built up habits of coloniality. These habits that trundle teleologically onward, without often pausing to either check coordinates of social, physical, and ethical locations, which profoundly compromise the potential for transformative change.

This book investigates the ways that educational research has been formed and regenerates itself as a deeply colonizing enterprise and then proposes epistemic changes for educational research from an anticolonial stance. My analysis speaks primarily to the most mainstream and financially well-supported educational research. I make substantive use of the processes used in doctoral programs, as these programs function as sites of apprenticeship, transparently and opaquely communicating the social, physical, and ethical values of academic educational research.

Assemblage of Locations

I offer this analysis by prioritizing attention to social locations, the unfixed yet durable histories and trajectories that incompletely structure what we know and how we know. I speak from several locations, personal and professional. Those locations are assemblages (Deleuze, 1995; Wyatt and Gale, 2013), unfixed and protean but distinct enough coordinates that manifest in an ability and responsibility to, in complex fashion (Gordon, 1997), articulate one's own referent points. I provide a brief gesture here of my own set of coordinates, to both provide you, the reader, with an idea of whose eyes you might catch a look through now and then, and also to manifest a stance of all knowledge, and therefore research, as ontological and situated, as coming from somewhere(s) and someone(s).

In part, I speak to you as the daughter of immigrants from South Asia. My parents' migration journey echoed state-sanctioned importing of intellectual capital across borders, reracialization in white-dominant spaces, and the maintenance of certain colonial structures such as gendered roles within and outside family life. My family succeeded and simultaneously failed within facile narratives of meritocracy and upward mobility. We embody a history of forced migration that yearns for settled and perhaps settler status while maintaining and mourning home practices. My history is one of interrupted relationship to land and culture, forced assimilation, and resistance to those cultural histories. Put simply, I am both colonizer and colonized. I understand the imperative of my specific social location to be in keeping with Dean Saranillio's point (2013) of "open[ing] one's visual world to the material consequences of aligning oneself with the settler state" (p. 282). These hybridities echo in many, as well as being thoroughly engendered in societal institutions. Coloniality, because of its pervasiveness, implicates everyone through its ongoing structure of people, land, and well-being. These implications do not mean that anyone's structural location relative to colonization is fixed by virtue of birthplace or social identity, but rather at every juncture there is constant opportunity and responsibility to identify and counter the genealogies of coloniality that continue to demand oppression. Specificity, then, offers a more robust potential for solidarity than eliding important differences in social locations (Gaztambide-Férnandez, 2012)

I also offer this writing as a lifelong educator who has taught in primary, secondary, and tertiary institutions, in the public and private realms for more than 20 years. I know a great deal about education and in many ways, learning remains torturously, beautifully elusive of a fixed definition for me. Learning is fundamentally a fugitive, transformative act. It runs from what was previously known, to become something not yet known. Terrifying and beautiful. Education, for centuries, within the grip of coloniality, has sought to make this essential aspect of humanness, learning and changing, definitively known. In its fundamental unknowability, learning can remind us of the limits of coloniality. It is from and within those histories that my own shifting relationship with educational research, anticolonial praxis, and answerability lives.

Wynter (2003) describes coloniality as core to the centuries-long projects of delineating statuses of humanity, and from those categories of human and not, the ability to own land and others. Coloniality has kept stable the core project of material domination, whether through religious- or state-defined delineations of worth. When decolonization is used metaphorically, then, as Tuck and Wayne Yang (2012) point out, the perhaps unintentional but still felt impact secures colonial structures by keeping relationships among being and land abstract and vague, paradoxically and dysfunctionally enabling an erasure of the roots and tendrils of coloniality.

The United States is a settler colony, and while other forms of colonization are present here, the primary structure of people, land, and relation is through settler colonialism (Byrd, 2011). Within the structure of settler colonialism, land is central. It is constantly pursued, a thirst that can never be satisfied, making ownership of land the fulcrum around which other relationships are formed. In part, because of the proliferation of the use of the decolonization (Tuck and Wayne Yang, 2012), I have opted to pause and more thoroughly explore its affordances, limits, as well as those of anticoloniality. In this sense, I use anticolonial in most of this book as a way to draw into relief the ways in which coloniality must be known to be countered, and decolonial should always address material changes. However, I also address decolonial moves that become available once anticolonial stances are enacted. This is a subtle yet important distinction – anticolonial and decolonial praxis is not consecutive, but to decolonize does require the apprehension and unsettling of coloniality.

While it is problematic to conceptualize decolonization as a stripping away of anything deemed nonNative because of it implications for maintaining essentialized identities and social locations (Grande, 2004; Lyons, 2010), it is a differentially problematic enterprise to speak to those potentials from a mix of forced migration and settler histories. I don't easily participate in decolonial conversations about how to free this Indigenous land from its settler colony structure as I am part of the history that has secured that status. However, neither would I expect a person of Indigenous descendancy to have rarified knowledge – let alone the complexities of what an Indigenous person is saddled with in terms of communicating Native epistemologies to nonNatives.

Such un-ease, such dis-ease, though, are not reasons to abdicate from participation wholesale. I reach beyond what I've known while staying mindful of how I've been socialized to know myself within a settler society. Precisely because I experience both spoils and subjugation through the settler colonial project, I must participate in the project of dismantling settler colonialism. I can speak to the ways that the histories and ongoing project of settler colonialism have shaped relationships, as that is part of how I have come to understand my own social locations.

In this text, I have pursued a critique of coloniality in its manifestation in educational research, as well as mapping terrain to how educational research has been, in some instances, and can be more answerable to learning and knowledge. However, no single text or practice can adequately decolonize any context. Most substantively, colonization is about material structures. Settler colonialism's fulcrum is the land; coloniality more broadly is about the stratification of beingness to serve accumulation of material and land. A text can make visible coloniality but it does not, in and of itself, shift material relations among human beings, including their connections to land (land here meaning land, air, water, and space) and other beings. Difficult questions and movements towards land repatriation and reparations, for example, are inherent to a full engagement with decolonization, and while Indigenous and colonized peoples should be central in articulating these various designs, because of the pervasive and historical reach of coloniality, no one can claim neutrality and therefore abstain. Any text and practice that aspires to be decolonial must be seen as a globally shared responsibility that is necessary but insufficient, as mapping these genealogies does not directly address the repatriation of land and alterations to material conditions. It is a shift of imagination.

This globally shared responsibility challenges contemporary conceptions of identity that tend to locate privilege and oppression within specific populations

(Grande, 2004). Even though it is undeniable that some people enjoy and wield settler status more pervasively, coloniality does not statically reside in some and not others. The structure is far too pervasive and therefore is more aptly countered by attending to the ways that we come into relation through coloniality. My history as a third world womanist, my relationship to the lands my family was pushed from and across borders to settle on, the practices that were maintained across these movements, and my commitment to teaching and learning runs throughout how I understand myself in relationship to knowledge and colonization. My approach is rooted in my own history, in keeping with anticolonial relationality as a way of being, and doing research, that challenges stratified relations and their reproduction of colonial structures in educational research and institutions.

Finally, my stance is undoubtedly my stance right now. True to any writing and thinking, as my own reading, understanding, and praxis around countering coloniality continues in relation to the context of educational research, I will certainly continue to pause and change my mind (Smith, 2010), particularly as I stay in conversation with others whose trajectories have been differently shaped by the structure of settler colonialism. At times, I have felt pauses as colleagues have conceptually tugged on my coat, urging me to think more or differently, and I in turn tug on others' coats in the same vein. Those pauses and shifts should not be seen as reasons to abstain from interacting but rather should shape how we read and understand all writing as temporally located. This stance, itself, is counter to coloniality and its myth of universal truth.

What, then, is beyond the current frames of colonial relationships? In fact, throughout history and in contemporary times, examples abound of spaces where people work in relation to each other and natural resources out of stances of self-determination, stewardship, and answerability. In the work of giants like Ella Baker and Bob Moses in the African American community, Linda Tuhiwai Smith and Graham Smith in Indigenous communities, Ronald Takaki and Arudhati Roy in third world contexts, knowledge and learning is actively claimed and tended to as a core human right. Much of this work begins from an assumption that communities that have been under the heel of colonization hold within them deeper resources and ways of being, refusing to be defined through the colonizer's terms. As Katherine McKittrick puts it, in the introduction to her edited volume addressing Sylvia Wynter's work, "Wynter's anticolonial vision is not, then, teleological – moving from colonial oppression outward and upward toward emancipation – but rather consists of knots of ideas and histories and narratives that can only be legible in relation to one another" (2015, p. 7).

If colonization is about ownership and territoriality for some at the expense of others, anticolonial stances must imagine still being in relation with each other but for survivance: in order to grow and to thrive from lived agency. Aashinaabe writer Gerald Vizenor (2008) argues in his book, *Survivance*, that while many people in the world are enamored with and obsessed by the concocted images of the Indian

– the simulations of Indigenous character and cultures as essential victims – Native survivance is an active sense of presence over historical absence, deracination, and oblivion. I listen to Vizenor's use of survivance and call for various populations to consider their relationship to thriving as a contribution to collective possibility. How could and should profited and profiteering settlers, reluctant and forced settlers, Native-born, indigenous, and immigrants understand and enact their relationships to knowledge and learning as acts of a collective countering of coloniality? As James Baldwin (1963) wrote, "We are capable of carrying a great burden, once we discover that the burden is reality and arrive where reality is."

References

Baldwin, J. (1963). *The Fire Next Time*. New York: Penguin.

Battiste, M. (2013). *Decolonizing Education: Nourishing the Learning Spirit*. Saskatoon, Canada: Purich Publishing.

Bonilla-Silva, E. (2009). *Racism without Racists: Color-blind Racism and the Persistence of Racial Inequality in America*. Third Edition. Lanham, MD: Rowman & Littlefield.

Byrd, J.A. (2011). *The Transit of Empire: Indigenous Critiques of Colonialism*. Minneapolis: University of Minnesota Press.

Deleuze, G. (1995). *Negotiations 1972–1990*. New York: Columbia University Press.

Desjarlait, R. (2011). Decolonization and "Occupy Wall Street," *Indian Country Today Media Network.com*. Accessed July 21, 2014 from: http://indiancountrytodaymedianetwork. com/2011/10/23/decolonization-and-occupy-wall-street.

Gaztambide-Fernández, R.A. (2012). Decolonization and the Pedagogy of Solidarity. *Decolonization: Indigeneity, Education & Society* 1(1): 41–67.

Gordon, A. (1997). *Ghostly Matters: Haunting and the Sociological Imagination*. Minneapolis, MN: University of Minnesota Press.

Grande, S. (2004). *Red Pedagogy: Native American Social and Political Thought*. Lanham, MD: Rowman & Littlefield.

Lanham, R.A. (2007). *The Economics of Attention: Style and Substance in the Age of Information*. Chicago: University of Chicago Press.

Lather, P. (1986). Research as Praxis. *Harvard Educational Review* 56(3): 257–277.

Lyons, S.R. (2010). *X-marks: Native Signatures of Assent*. Minneapolis, MN: University of Minnesota Press.

McKittrick, K. (Ed.) (2015). *Sylvia Wynter: On Being Human as Praxis*. Chapel Hill, NC: Duke University Press.

Patel, L. (2013). *Youth Held at the Border: Immigration, Education, and the Politics of Inclusion*. New York: Teachers College Press.

Perry, I. (2011). *More Beautiful and More Terrible: The Embrace and Transcendence of Racial Inequality in the United States*. New York: NYU Press.

Ronson, J. (2015). *So You've Been Publicly Shamed*. New York: Penguin.

Saranillio, D.I. (2013). Why Asian Settler Colonialism Matters: A Thought Piece on Critiques, Debates, and Indigenous Difference. *Settler Colonial Studies* 3(3–4): 280–294.

Shahjahan, R.A. (2014). Being "Lazy" and Slowing Down: Toward Decolonizing Time, Our Body, and Pedagogy. *Educational Philosophy and Theory* 47(5): 488–501.

Smith, Z. (2010). *Changing My Mind: Occasional Essays*. Reprint Edition. New York: Penguin Books.

Tuck, E. (2009). Suspending Damage: A Letter to Communities. *Harvard Educational Review* 79(3): 409–428.

Tuck, E., and M. McKenzie (2015). *Place in Research: Theory, Methodology, and Methods.* New York: Routledge.

Tuck, E., and K. Wayne Yang (2012). Decolonization Is Not a Metaphor. *Decolonization: Indigeneity, Education & Society* 1(1). Accessed April 15, 2014 from: http://decolonization. org/index.php/des/article/view/18630.

Vizenor, G. (Ed.) (2008). *Survivance: Narratives of Native Presence.* Lincoln, NE: University of Nebraska Press.

Wyatt, J., and K. Gale (2013). Getting Out of Selves: An Assemblage/Ethnography. In: S. Holman Jones, T.E. Adams and C. Ellis (Eds.), *Handbook of Autoethnography.* Walnut Creek, CA: Left Coast Press.

Wynter, S. (2003). Unsettling the Coloniality of Being/Power/Truth/Freedom: Towards the Human, after Man, Its Overrepresentation – an Argument. *Centennial Review* 3(3): 257–337.

1

EDUCATIONAL RESEARCH AS A SITE OF COLONIALITY

Colonize: [kol-uh-nahyz] to form a colony, to settle in a colony.

Education, like the institutions and societies it derives from, is neither culturally neutral nor fair. Rather, education is a culturally and socially constructed institution for an imagined context with purposes defined by those who are privileged to be the deciders, and their work has not always been for the benefit of the masses [understatement]. Education has its roots in a patriarchal, Eurocentric society, complicit with multiple forms of oppression of women, sometimes men, children, minorities, and Indigenous peoples.

(Battiste, 2013, p. 159)

It is a quotidian observation that inequity exists. Sometimes this is expressed as inequality, typically manifested and tallied through a liberal democratic epistemology of single unit, single right or voice or count. Other times, the inequity is expressed as difference in relative amounts of power, status, and freedom. And, there are, of course, various attachments, tolerations, and revulsions to inequity. The social sciences are replete with various epistemic stances to equity, power, and justice.

But inequity is less understood as a material condition of which dominant and less frequent meanings are made and which meanings in turn are constantly shaping and reshaping material conditions. As Karen Barad (2007) proposes more broadly, meaning and matter are always entangled, coming into being, shifting, solidifying, colliding, and coalescing. Related sentiments have been expressed for longer and differently, by various thinkers from often-marginalized cultures, including, to name just a few, Indigenous scholar Oscar Kawagley and his work on ethnoecology, the Black feminist traditions of Akasha Hull, and third world womanist work by Arundhati Roy. Across these works is a refusal that word, meaning, and matter are immutably separate. What we say, think, and do is always already intertwined yet not finalized. This presents a distinct challenge to the idea of studying and learning from established knowledge systems and then engaging in practice. If we understand the published works themselves, the words, to have shaped what is materially available to do and practice, then how do we engage necessarily more dynamically? How do we make sense of, metaphorically and literally, inequitable material conditions. How does materially lived inequity influence the meanings we make? And finally, if our only ways of interacting with contexts are through ongoing projects of coloniality and even deconstructions of colonialism, how can we enliven possibilities and futurities outside of these conditions?

At its core, research is about the pursuit of knowledge. In this book, I focus on the ways that coloniality is manifested in both material conditions and the meanings that are made of those conditions, specifically within the field of educational research, and particularly what this structure means for projects of decolonization. In this chapter, I propose a relatively simple premise: that education research, through both meaning and matter, has played a deleterious role in perpetuating and refreshing colonial relationships among people, practices, and land. This is not to say this is the only purpose that educational research has performed, nor that all educational researchers are colonizers themselves. Rather, it means that logics of coloniality, which are connected to property and stratifications of society, are problematically enlivened through educational research.

I open this chapter by making use of Jared Diamond's popular treatise of why things [matter] are the way they are to then propose an alternative stance to making meaning and effecting matter. I then carry this engagement with knowledge about learning to educational research. I begin with Diamond not so much to position his work as particularly central to knowledge and learning but to illustrate, through example, that knowledge and meanings always have material consequences, and in so understanding, these dynamics are rendered more open and permeable to epistemic alterity.

Why Are Things the Way They Are?

In Jared Diamond's massively popular book, *Guns, Germs, and Steel* (1999), the geographer commences with a relatively straightforward question: why is it that some civilizations conquered others? Explicitly rejecting the premise that conquering occurs by virtue of racial superiority and inferiority, Diamond traces the history of 13,000 years of civilizations. Through this history, he details the gaps in power and technologies between human societies, largely attributing advancement in power to differences in environmental geography and humans' uses of that geography. Environmental differences such as communicable diseases and humans' domestication of animals are explored not just as singular factors but intertwined aspects of civilizations that have had relative amounts of success and strength. Diamond also explores, to a much lesser extent, the role of writing, literacy, and ideas.

> Writing marched together with weapons, microbes, and centralized political organization as a modern agent of conquest. The commands of the monarchs and merchants who organized colonizing fleets were conveyed in writing. The fleets set their courses by maps and written sailing directions prepared by previous expeditions. Written accounts of earlier expeditions motivated later ones, by describing the wealth and fertile lands awaiting the conquerors. The accounts taught subsequent explorers what conditions to expect, and helped them prepare themselves. The resulting empires were administered with the aid of writing. While all of those types of information were also transmitted by other means in preliterate societies, writing made the transmission easier, more detailed, more accurate, and more persuasive.
>
> (p. 215)

I draw attention to Diamond's brief discussion of textual practices for several reasons. First, all language is, to a certain extent, metaphorical and therefore representative, a signifier of something else (Derrida, 1973; Grande, 2014), and all texts and textual practices are socially and culturally situated. As Marie Battiste (2013) articulates in her book, *Decolonizing Education*, schools, pivotal locations of textual learning are never neutral sites. Linda Tuhiwai Smith also details clearly in the classic, *Decolonizing Methodologies*, how research has never been neutral. It is not difficult to see contemporary echoes of what Diamond portends, that "written accounts of earlier expeditions motivated later ones." Educational research is a text, and as such, is never neutral but instead imbricated with potential and unruliness to motivate, disincentivize, and render invisible various realities. In fact, all texts, whether written, oral, or physical, carry contextually situated meanings and those meanings interact with materiality, for more and less desirable outcomes. That Diamond pays such little attention, though, to the ways that epistemologies, the ways that peoples viewed conquest, war, and domination, were communicated, upheld, and challenged, presents a profound lost opportunity to situate matters as intimately tied to meaning, an omission that may also apply to some educational research.

In fact, Diamond's work has come under justifiable fire for many different reasons, including a simplistic view of some cultures, a questionable reduction of many complex histories of conquest into the singular node of agriculture, and pat recommendations for addressing the devouring of the planet's resources. One of the key criticisms, though, is one integral to this book: that humans' relation to matter is pivotal to colonial, neocolonial, and potentially decolonial stances. As Jason Antrosio (2013) said, "What Diamond glosses over is that just because you have guns and steel does not mean you should use them for colonial and imperial purposes." In other words, while Diamond thoroughly documents geographic and environmental differences, his light treatment of attitudes towards these material resources elides the role that a colonizing worldview plays in how human beings decide to be in relation with each other, the land, and its resources. This is a substantive omission, as worldviews are ways of manifesting ethics and values. For Diamond to avoid direct confrontation of imperialism as a worldview is one thing. That his work is wildly and widely popular also tells us something about collective will to engage with and disassociate from the ongoing project of colonialism and imperialism.

What makes Diamond popular is, in part, what scholars Eve Tuck and K. Wayne Yang call a "move to innocence," an absence that creates a justified presence of ownership, of colonial territory. In Tuck and Wayne Yang's (2012) work, they cite and indict moves to innocence as one of the ways that colonial violence is mythologized as past histories to secure ongoing protected privilege. A now classic example of this is how both the attempted genocide of Indigenous peoples and the anti-blackness era of Jim Crow are taught as historical moments, when in fact, both projects have continued with force (Alexander, 2012; Smith, 2011). The material and meaningful impact of Diamond's work being so widely read is parallel: consumer sanction of Diamond's work collectively validates ellipses on the intentional colonial framework of domination. It is endorsed through its absence and preferred geopolitical happenstance-like attention on agriculture, technology, and disease, which can all be more comfortably engaged with a lack of intentionality, allowing for an erasure of genealogies of these traditions. This, even though writing and communication in many of the conquering cultures that Diamond explored, from the start, explicitly served the material and ideological purposes of the transit of empire (Byrd, 2011; Wynter, 2003).

How we make meaning of material conditions and our actions, study them, and communicate those findings is inextricably bound up with the ongoing project of coloniality as well as potentials to interrupt it and other ways of knowing and learning. Like Diamond's work, this book is concerned with the question of why it is that within conquering/conquered societies, Western(ized) societies in particular, there are perpetuating and perpetuated differences in educational achievement among populations along racial and ethnic lines. Why is it that long after colonization has occurred through the intentional use of guns, germs, and steel to colonize, colonized peoples, now sharing physical space with those who colonized them, remain at the lower end of the social system in terms of access to security, health, and wealth, and experience the daily impacts of systemic violence? Further, how is this oppression tolerated and maintained in nations/states like the United States, that profess ideals of equality and freedom? However, unlike Diamond's work, the inquiry into material differences views materiality as intimately connected to meanings, to the knowledge that is produced about material conditions and how that knowledge creates material conditions.

Here the core focus is on knowledge and learning, how the colonial state sanctions certain forms of knowledge and reifies projects of learning that don't actually often have to do with learning or relationships to knowledge, and how those (per)form and reseat colonial sets of relationships. Within that inquiry into coloniality is the under-explored role of educational research as symptomatic, emblematic, and beholden to coloniality. In this way, I attempt to take up DuBois' (1898) call to "reverse the gaze."

When W.E.B. DuBois (1898) was commissioned in the 1890s to investigate, as his funders put it, the negro [sic] problem in Philadelphia, he undertook one of the first studies of racial disparities, and used quantitative and qualitative data to focus not just on Black populations but also their contexts, verily helping to establish the field of sociology, though he is rarely credited with this. He used tools and analysis that we might now categorize as anthropological and sociological, "reveal[ing] the Negro group as a symptom, not a cause; as a striving, palpitating group, and not an inert, sick body of crime; as a long historic development and not a transient occurrence" (p. 175). DuBois looked to Black populations and their vulnerabilized positions in society as a symptom of that society. This stance was in active opposition to what he was commissioned to study, which was, colloquially put, what was wrong with those Black folks.

Taking that cue, I seek to locate education research specifically within its societal contexts, particularly the context of ongoing colonialism and its deep need for differences that can be ranked and used to study disparities. What do we, as social science researchers, have to do with these disparities? In what ways are our actions, research questions, and foci symptomatic and even perhaps protective of the larger context of disparity and colonization? What are the ways that the material work and meanings made through educational research support coloniality and what are the possibilities for work outside of coloniality? From a view of education as a system, the practices of researchers, teachers, and policymakers have fluid interaction with the centuries-long processes that foment the privileged and the oppressed, the colonizers and the colonized, the vaulted and the marginalized. It is from this stance that I invite myself and other education researchers to contend with our places in an iniquitous system that has amassed, and is itself invested in, a collective educational debt. Education research is not removed from this system. In fact, how could it be? Formal education and research have existed and thrived as part of a larger colonial project since the first establishment of schools in the colonies (Lomawaima and McCarty, 2006). We should, in fact, expect that colonialism will be pervasively experienced, wrought upon, and tightly protected, almost regardless of what our ethical stances on oppression might be.

But most often, questions about ethics in human subjects research are collapsed (Tuck and Guishard, 2013) and circumscribed to institutionally driven procedures of informed consent that ritualize the appearance of "giving voice" to others (Wilson, 2008). Rarely are conversations engaged about the ethics and responsibilities of educational research as itself part of a system that perpetuates inequities through schooling and research about schooling.

Higher Education and Education as Reflection of Colonial Ideologies

In the United States, education figures prominently within the public imaginary as deliverance from iniquities in society. Even amidst overwhelming evidence of the complexity in what contributes to social stability and mobility, education maintains its central place. Ever fond of sports metaphors, Americans often colloquially refer to education as the way to "level the playing field," meaning that while children may be born into differential environments, education can enable individuals to transcend the scripts of those environments. When President Barack Obama introduced Sonia Sotomayor as his nominee for the United States Supreme Court, he highlighted her triumph over low odds for achievement, and attributed her success to studying hard in her Brooklyn schools and maintaining that ethic through Ivy League college and law school (Obama, 2009). Even though in her own memoir, Justice Sotomayor (2013) tells a much more complicated narrative of opportunity, chance, and gendered roles, her nomination was politically framed through the more palatable and simpler myth of education as a relay for meritocracy. This widely held belief in the promise of education is echoed in policies and governmental actions. In the United States, access to a free and public education has been negotiated by various groups and awarded as a symbol of this opportunity (*Brown v. Board of Education of Topeka*, 1954; *Lau v. Nichols*, 1974). In fact, national progress in civil rights is almost always examined, in part, through the contours of equity and inequity within the field of education (e.g., Rumberger and Palardy, 2005). And by that measure of educational opportunity and success, the report card is and has been dismal for hundreds of years in this and other colonial societies (Battiste, 2013; Castagno and Brayboy, 2008; Lomawaima and McCarty, 2006).

Inequity in education is both so ubiquitous and so persistent that we have a nickname for it, the achievement gap, our shorthand for the disparity on educational measures between groups of students. Particularly entrenched have been the gaps between white students and their peers of color, most often mentioned are African American and Latino youth. Conduct a Google search for the achievement gap and you will find results numbering over 1.5 million. If you limit your search to scholar.google.com, a search engine for academic papers, your search will be somewhat more confined, to just under a million entries of research that explore the achievement gap, ways to close this gap, and implications for educators. Educational researchers have become recipients of doctorates, received tenure, been promoted, honored, and lauded for studying this gap. The gap remains. I question what functions and dysfunctions are being served by this gap, and an associative, seemingly unassailable frame that the gap can actually be closed without confronting coloniality and its key strategies. More directly, what does educational research have to do not just with the gap in achievement but also securing and perpetuating legacies of colonization? Where is education research transcribed into and therefore beholden to maintaining the achievement gap?

Toward a Systemic View of Educational Inequity

In her 2006 Presidential address to the American Educational Research Association, Gloria Ladson-Billings called upon educational researchers to shift their lenses from the achievement gap to the education debt. A debt is something that is owed; a gap can simply exist. A debt raises questions of who owes whom and who stands to benefit, and surfaces questions of equity. A gap can be seen to be merely occurring and rectifiable with some kind of filler, but not necessitating a shift in the core conditions that created the gap. Through this one-word change, Ladson-Billings calls upon educational research to widen and deepen the ways in which educational disparities are framed.

Ladson-Billings traces the path of Native, African American, Latino, and Asian immigrant children in the United States and posits that it is through moral, sociopolitical, and historical debts that educational standing must be viewed. To measure the yearly changes on test scores gives a slice of information, and to only tell those scores demands a decontextualized view of "achievement" that normalizes the top achievers, in this case white middle class students, as natural and desired. But to contextualize the scores from a debt perspective begs consideration of intertwined socio-economic, political, and colonial factors that work together to justify white middle and upper class culture as exceptional. As Ladson-Billings (2006) explains in just one example from her Presidential address, "Indeed, Black students in the South did not experience universal secondary schooling until 1968 ... Why, then, would we not expect there to be an achievement gap?" When situated within histories of economic, sociopolitical, and moral blockages to education, we can see that the test scores only begin to represent one outcropping of the education debt that this nation and others like it are accruing.

Although Ladson-Billings does not term it as such, she is asking educational researchers to regard both educational disparities and how those disparities are framed as symptomatic of a larger system. In this book, I use system and holistic to mean the ways in which dynamic systems of human and nonhuman life forms function in material contexts. All collectives operate in systems, but the kind of collective differs across contexts. In an interlocking system that is structured on coloniality (Wynter, 2003), the advancement of some rests upon the required disenfranchisement of others. Within a competitive, capitalistic society, there can be no winners without losers, no black market without a white market (Schlosser, 2012), no white privilege without accompanying anti-blackness. Geographer David Harvey (2003) has analyzed and theorized the ways that this conjoining has led to, in the shape of capitalism since the 1970s, racialized accumulation through dispossession. The reach of this system is far and deep, into law, education, health, and interpersonal relationships (Collins, 2009).

When Ladson-Billings implores her audience to consider educational debt, and not more benignly and inaccurately construed as a gap, she brings attention to not just one aspect of the social system, as is most often the case, but several aspects of the system over time and place. A gap can make more sense as a descriptor if one is interested in finding a cause–effect solution to a single problem and in reifying a worldview that equity is in fact not just possible empirically but simply held at bay in the given context. In reality, it is understandable that social science has often focused on single factors, given its relationship to science as being defined through single factor analyses that had been established in studies of individuals through psychology and through federal granting structures that reinforced and rewarded such frames (Lagemann, 2002). Ladson-Billings puts the resultant and deficit-compatible frame of the achievement gap in the context of structured inequity. She highlights legal restrictions from formal education, abysmal per-pupil spending in low-income contexts, and consistent informal disenfranchisement of communities and parents of color. These practices accumulate over centuries and interact with each other dynamically to compose a purposefully stratified and inequitable system. From such a view, conversations and research studies about which factor we should isolate and alter to close the achievement gap are, in terms of efficacy and transformation, over before they have begun. The system is, in many ways, doing exactly what it is designed to do, which is to segment land, people, and relationships among them into strata. When educational research focuses on these strata without addressing the societal design that creates the strata, it becomes complicit in the larger project. It may temporarily improve a small set of experiences, often conceptualized with gaining footholds on a slanted wall, rather than reconsidering the entire structure. In other words, if we are not reckoning with the legacies of sociopolitical practices that have created and are created by our practices, including the disparities of achievement on assessments, how can we hope to alter those practices? The practices that lead some to carry educational debt are interwoven with the practices that lead others to educational opportunity and wealth. This relationship of wealth and debt can be obscured by silo investigations and interventions that aim to fill the gap but not address its fundamental conditions. Part of what decolonizing educational research must include is understanding how an imbalanced and misreferenced partial view, fundamentally, works from a colonial stance.

Colonial Parts and Holism

As scholar Marie Ann Battiste reminds her readers, in *Decolonizing Education*, compartmentalizing a whole into disparate parts is endemic to colonization and control. Contrastingly, Indigenous knowledge systems view life and being as holistic, complex, and interdependent. Battiste quotes Willie Ermine's work:

> The year 1492 marked the first meeting of two disparate world-views, each on its own uncharted course of exploration and discovery for purposeful knowledge. The encounter featured two diametric trajectories into the realm of knowledge. One was bound for uncharted destination in outer

space, the physical, and the other was on a delicate path into inner space, the metaphysical.

(as quoted in Battiste, 2013, p. 160)

Compartmentalizing complex wholes into disparate pieces facilitates the naming and ordering of those pieces and parts in order to have dominion over them. Dating back to the 16th century expansion of church power and conquest, expressions of the "truth" of human existence relied upon delineating who was human and who was not; in other words, partitioning diverse and complex life forms into non-permeable categories (Wynter, 2003). Those categories, and keeping them separate, are inextricably necessary for the colonial project of naming and sorting for the purpose of metering worth and safety while also justifying disparities as part of a natural order. With holistic order broken into different pieces and the majority focus on those parts, it is more difficult to challenge assumptions about the overall system.

This is not to say that inquiry into individual parts has no place or, more so, only a colonial role in research. Deep and expert knowledge is entirely necessary to the health and well-being of any heterogeneous whole. Myriad examples exist for when and how we consult experts because they are experts and have more than a passing knowledge of their discipline. Care must be taken to not interpret this critique of colonial partitioning as any kind of anti-intellectualism that seeks to denigrate the need for experts in specific practices, processes, and knowledges. To determine the presence of coloniality in dividing up wholes into parts, I attend to the relation and purpose to that division. As mentioned before, Sylvia Wynter (2003) mapped the ways that gradations of virtually everything, but most intensely the heavens, land, and living beings, were named thusly to determine ownership of and ability to claim truth. Coloniality created projects of knowledge for the purposes of segmenting and the overriding ability to segment, to own the truth about the parts. The earth was seen as gradations away from the heavens, in the view of the church, and some lands therein were designated as holier, worthier than others. This sort of division into parts may well allow for close-up inspection and study of those parts, but the overall knowledge project is contaminated by the relation to what might be studied and who can conduct that study. In coloniality, divisions and gradations are necessary in order to have greater and lesser amounts of control and power over those divisions. When, in the social sciences, we say that we are controlling for x, y, and z factors of human existence, we are appealing to a hubris that complexly lived realities can be partitioned and controlled, and we do so for the sake of proclaiming a truth about the factor that we believe we have isolated. This critique is nothing new and has been part of the appeal of the complexity sciences (e.g., Geyer and Bogg, 2007), which themselves have been taken up and used within educational studies (Davis and Sumara, 2009; McQuillan, 2008). However, the work of Sylvia Wynter and other scholars of coloniality brings forward the question of the function of these knowledge projects and their focus on parts. A focus on the part from a stance of prediction and causality runs the risk of disallowing transgressive and productive knowledge across parts, across disciplinary walls, and across traditions.

I believe we must, rather boldly, see what correlations, connections, and causations we, as sanctioned producers of knowledge about learning, hold in these disparities. We must do so with an intentional reckoning with the worldviews used to formulate, conduct, and share research, specifically about education and learning.

Architecture for Apprentices

In the interest of understanding and stewarding complexity and holism, I ask how educational research makes use of studying parts at the expense of the whole and how that has facilitated a trend to misframe and misresearch inequity. Within the field of educational research, my inquiry focuses particularly upon the genre of research, how it facilitates certain kinds of meaning through what is written, received, and positioned favorably. Within contemporary societies, knowledge and power are inextricably linked, most often through writing and speaking. From educational policies to educational research, the lived material realities of today's youth, their families, and their teachers are permeated by and intricately influenced by texts. How we write about, study, enact legislation and policies, and assess children, is all based in writing and some of the texts. Consider the texts that precede university-sanctioned research, the texts that doctoral students must produce on their way to becoming institutionally recognized educational researchers:

• Development of literature reviews of existing research on a topic.
• Review of methodologies used to study the topic in the past.
• Development of a written research proposal, typically including a problem statement, literature review, theoretical framework, methods, and significance or implications of the study.
• Proposal to an Institutional Review Board to conduct human subjects research.

Not a single piece of data has been collected, but it is within these texts that, already, who should be studied, and by whom and how, is defined. In fact, these processes are meant to be tantamount to exploring and addressing ethical concerns that may arise from research involving human subjects. By following these steps, it is as though we are operating outside of an unequal system, a system that echoes and rebirths legacies of colonization. Beyond research proposals and extending into research studies, their findings, school curricula, and policies, these textual practices have material consequences for people at various points in the system, including educational researchers. It is within the genre of academic research, then, that I look to investigate the role of educational research in the continued systemic disenfranchisement of populations.

To understand how the genre of academic research works, it is instructive to look closely at where openings exist for newcomers; stages where novices, graduate students, are being apprenticed into the academy. In Lave and Wenger's (1991) touchstone piece that illuminated the ways that learning occurs within communities, legitimate peripheral participation (LPP) was highlighted as a fundamental route to full inclusion and practice within the group. It was in those LPP spaces that productive trial and error occurred. Similarly, the academy might be best understood from the ways that it teaches, implicitly and explicitly, what is legitimate participation. In terms of becoming a social science scholar, this participation takes place within the field of doctoral studies.

As part of this apprenticeship, doctoral students take courses in research methodologies to study the ways in which research knowledge is framed, gathered, and communicated. These research practices, along with knowledge about what counts as a valid research topic, are then put forth in doctoral dissertations. The dissertation acts as a sort of academic calling card for newly minted PhDs (Kilbourn, 2006), communicating to members of the academy that the doctoral candidate is capable of academic research and writing, and that their work contributes original knowledge to the field of educational research, and is rigorous in its design and findings. However, from a different stance, a stance in which the gaze is turned back onto educational research, doctoral dissertations also mirror what the field deems worthy. This worthiness is bestowed only by those who have already passed the traditional requirements of doctoral work. Doctoral students engage in these practices not only as passive receptacles of genres and conventions but also because they understand these practices to be aligned with future career prospects.

In the following section, I explore the work of contemporary doctoral dissertations to illuminate the ways in which a research question says a great deal about what preceded it and about the keys needed to unlock the gates to the academy. I remind myself and the reader that this analysis is done with humility and hope; that although some of this may sting, it is necessary for healing to occur. This analysis, then, is not so much about the dissertations themselves, but more about the system of educational research that condones, even requires, these forms of colonizing knowledge.

Where Does a Question Come From?

In his oratory introduction to KRS-One's audio CD, *Ruminations*, Professor Cornel West (2003) pushes his audience of higher education students to consider where a question comes from.

> Those cast in the arbitrary constructs of brown, black, yellow, red are inferior, less beautiful, less intelligent. What a lie, but, my God, that lie has taken on tremendous ferocity. [pause] And it's still around. Who cares about the intelligence of those with blue eyes as opposed to those with brown eyes? You can't get a PhD in psychology from that. Who cares

about the intelligence of those in Georgia as opposed to those in North Dakota? You can't get a dissertation in psychology studying that! But you raise black and white, and that's a very serious issue. I know it's going to be delicate for some of you [laughter], but let's see what the evidence shows. That's how science works. [pause] Where does a question come from?

In the years from 2004 to 2009, 909 dissertations were completed and published that included one of the following terms in the title: achievement gap, African American or Black students, African American or Black youth, Latino students, Latino youth, immigrant students, immigrant youth, at-risk students, at-risk youth, marginalized students, and marginalized youth. Within those studies, most of the dissertation titles focus on one population and one factor or characteristic relative to that population and/or its learning experiences. For example, in Asterilla's (2008) dissertation entitled, "The Fragments of Frustration in Building Academic Literacy for College-Bound African-American Students: Implications for the Use of Outdoor Education," we see a focus upon college-bound African American students and an investigation into outdoor education for building academic literacy. But where does this question come from? This research inquiry, quite logically, emanates from a system in which academic literacy is often falsely equated with intelligence (Lemke, 1997), in which first Native Americans and then African Americans, etc., are disenfranchised from a cultural model of literacy that is the home of the white middle class (Lee, 2005), and from a research industrial complex in which interventions are common as the solution to the achievement "gap."

The same focus on interventions is within the work of seasoned researchers, who, rather than just having cleared the hurdles of graduate study, are actively engaged in foundation-sponsored research into the achievement gap. In Biancarosa and Snow's (2004) Carnegie-sponsored report on how to move beyond the early literacy foci of recent U.S. national educational agendas and address secondary learners, they state:

> In addition, the problems faced by struggling readers are exacerbated when they do not speak English as their first language, are recent immigrants, or have learning disabilities. Indeed, a struggling reader may fit all three of these descriptions, making intervention a truly complicated proposition.
>
> (p. 9)

Here, outdoor education as an intervention might not pass muster, as there are several different factors that may cause a reader to struggle. Within these two examples from a novice and more experienced researchers, we see that the underlying logic of educational research is to locate the factor affecting the population and then home in on a single intervention. Research produces knowledge that assesses the single intervention and projects implications for its use with other populations. How might research progress differently if it searched for interventions to transform the interconnected structures that marginalize some populations while privileging others? Reversing the gaze in this fashion would render single interventions less than adequate. Rightly so, the quest for a technical intervention becomes appropriately stunted when it is a colonially defined social system and not just a group of individuals in need of an intervention.

However, simply increasing the number of factors being considered does not necessarily bring in a more systemic view of the marginalized and privileged. In Asterilla's (2008) dissertation, we have now several factors that might speak to the achievement of African American urban youth. Without a doubt, stress, confidence, and parental involvement interact dynamically with academic achievement, and an inquiry into this dynamic is certainly more ecologically grounded than a study into just one of the factors. Nowhere in the title of this dissertation, though, do we gain an understanding of the ways that a discriminatory society produces stress, reduces confidence, and often precludes involvement of parents in educational institutions. In other words, seizing upon more conditions is not the equivalent of seizing upon the root (N. Drane, personal communication, 2015). Without naming the discriminatory and racist society in which African American urban youth live, the system is silenced, and the target of the intervention (to reduce stress, build confidence, and involve parents) is solely articulated for/upon the youth, not the context in which they live. In other words, the meaning that is being made leaves the material conditions uninterrogated, in many ways securing those material conditions. Although interventions for individuals and systems need not be diametrically opposed, my concern is that rarely is there is an intervention for the racist society predicated on colonization, while interventions abound for marginalized populations to bridge the gap between themselves and privileged populations. While these interventions proliferate, and the researchers documenting them solidify their positions in society. The most vulnerable populations remain vulnerable to a society that is poised, at best, to assimilate them into dominant cultural practices, and more typically, to keep them in low-income and less safe contexts.

Imagine an alternate inquiry into stress, confidence, and parental involvement, but this time with the population of legacy college attendees at elite private colleges and universities. No such study exists, or anything remotely similar to it, in the 909 dissertations completed over the last five years on the achievement gap. Only the "at-risk," those in need of intervention are studied, those who are in the preferential spots in society are generally not studied, and because of that silencing, they are re-centered as the norm. Those struggling are spotlighted as the area of need, not a colonial structure that arranges all the participants into their respective spots. Only in recent years have high-achieving populations been studied, but this has been with an eye to downwardly apply these practices as interventions for those who haven't succeeded (Duckworth, Peterson, Matthews, and Kelly, 2007). The implicit working theory in this research agenda is that those who have succeeded in society have done so because of a discernible cluster of characteristics, and not due to sociopolitical systems of privilege and oppression. It is related to a stance that would seek to pin the unabashed use of stop and frisk law enforcement policies with Black and Latino populations (Peart, 2011) on how they dress (e.g., baggy pants) rather than systemic and pervasive anti-blackness. The cumulative effect of this framing is that a colonial context, which deeply needs strata to inequitably divide up wealth and resources, is maintained. Despite the vicissitudes of damage to the planet and its inhabitants that have come into existence because of capitalism-fueled colonial stances, those who hold the most power in exacting these conditions are rarely seen as in need of intervention. The privileged need no intervention; they have already achieved. These practices of achievement are so normalized that they are invisible, not worthy of inquiry, and certainly not seen as dynamically connected to the populations that are poor, incarcerated, suffering, and displaced.

From this line of logic, the interventions that abound in the thousands of other studies into oppressed populations (sometimes known as at-risk, marginalized, or, quite euphemistically, urban) are designed for those populations to achieve like attendees at the private elite college. Rarely do the interventions directly address the ways in which status is so inequitably conferred. Nor do social scientists actually consider the plausibility of how an iniquitous social order, established through privilege and disenfranchisement, can structurally close the gap between the haves and the have-nots. Put another way, how are we theorizing that this society, borne of settler colonialism (Tuck and Wayne Yang, 2012; Wolfe, 1999) and structured on racism and class stratification, will easily morph to a society beyond frames of haves and have-nots?

Ladson-Billings' call to consider educational debt flips a facile and obscuring frame of the achievement gap on its head. I extend upon this necessarily revised frame to then situate research into inequities from a sociopolitical perspective. Without a consistent and explicit exploration of the systemic factors that are institutionalized into the daily rhythm of oppressed and privileged peoples, social scientists reflect and become part of that system that is built on inequity and injustice. Even more radical would be a research stance that used holistic ecologies as the default from and into which meanings are made and practices conducted, with foci on single parts as fundamentally incomplete. Examples for reckoning with the intertwined nature of living beings and material contexts exist. With each, though, there are different stances on how those connections are understood and effected.

Complex Wholes and Interconnectivity

Examples for starting with a reckoning of the intertwined nature of humans and contexts exist. In the video, *Unnatural Causes* (California Newsreel, 2008) the episode "When the Bough Breaks" charts the search for explanations of disproportionately high incidences of infant mortality and low birth weight of children of African American mothers. By contrast to babies of U.S.-born white American mothers, babies from African American mothers are four times more likely to be premature and three times more likely to die before their first birthday. The rates are alarming, disturbing. What could be the cause? The documentary progresses as the following factors are successively discussed and dismissed: genetics, socio-economic level, and country of origin. Using large-scale quantitative data, the health researchers profiled in the video make the case that what seemed most logical to the medical field, genetics and socio-economic level, cannot explain the prevalence of low birth weight and high infant mortality rates in babies born to African American mothers. To illustrate the case, the documentary focuses particularly closely on the history of a successful African American lawyer and the medical complications of her daughter, born prematurely and with a birth weight low enough to relegate her to a neo-natal unit for the first month of her life. As this woman talks over images of her now-healthy daughter and recounts how she had followed all the advised practices of eating well and resting during her pregnancy, the viewer is left with the question of how this healthy, economically stable woman gave birth to a premature and delicate infant. The medical experts unfold their history of inquiry into cases like the lawyer's, investigating and successively ruling out the factors of genetics and socio-economic status. They highlight that the only remaining possibility was to look for what African American women, and not African or white American women, had in common, and that was the shared context of a discriminatory society. Revamped in focus, the studies conducted under this view of African American women in a racist and sexist society investigated the role of societal toxins and stress. Over time, the human system that runs high on the stress from daily experiences of discrimination manifests this stress biophysically. One researcher likened the accumulation of these daily stresses to constantly revving a car engine; the integrity of the engine will begin to show the signs of undue wear and tear, of abuse.

Although the documentary spoke predominantly of the experiences of racism, the women also surely experienced intersectional oppression (Crenshaw, 1993), through both racism and sexism. Systems biologists now routinely consider the ways in which multiple systems: neurological, genetic, physical, and cultural, all interact dynamically with each other to produce particular human practices, behaviors, and tendencies. This extra-education inquiry provides an elegant but simple example of the fact that interior and external worlds are in dynamic relationship with each other. Parts within a whole cannot be understood without dynamic, complex views that are considerate of the legacies of colonialism and oppression.

Education research that segments populations by characteristics, deems them at-risk, and designs and tests interventions for them may provide short-term bandages for the flow of blood from colonizing legacies, but this research also ultimately works to sustain the system and how it confers safety and status. These more implicit echoes of coloniality are no less potent; rather, they are more insidious because they co-opt populations into looking first and solely to themselves for explanations to the question of why they are not succeeding, practices that Marie Battiste (2013) calls cognitive imperialism. The African American mother profiled in *Unnatural Causes* was perplexed by the low birth weight of her daughter, wondering what *she* had done wrong. Similarly, populations disenfranchised at the hands of formalized schooling typically look to themselves first to explain their lower status, a process of internalization that, as Tuck puts it, works in the specific and cumulatively so that disenfranchised communities come to see themselves as damaged (Tuck, 2009). This is echoed and perpetuated in educational research that provides a seemingly endless stream of interventions for "at-risk" populations. In this way, educational research is often complicit in a system that normalizes the achievement and wealth of some while pathologizing and marginalizing others. For decades upon decades, educational research has operated in this fashion. The roots of this vantage point are found, not surprisingly, in the establishment of the U.S. nation and are part and parcel of what fuels both function and dysfunction in educational research. Like all texts, educational research and its prevalent knowledge systems have a genealogy, a conduit through which some meanings have been protected and privileged for specific purposes. In the next chapter, I provide a more cohesive analysis of educational research as part of settler colonialism.

References

Alexander, Michelle (2012). *The New Jim Crow: Mass Incarceration in the Age of Colorblindness*. New York: The New Press.

Antrosio, J. (2013). Real History versus Guns, Germs and Steel. Accessed June 18, 2013 from: *Living Anthropologically*, www.livinganthropologically.com/anthropology/guns-germs-and-steel.

Asterilla, G.H.R. (2008). *The Fragments of Frustration in Building Academic Literacy for College-bound African-American Students: Implications for the Use of Outdoor Education*, Doctoral dissertation, George Mason University.

Barad, Karen (2007). *Meeting the Universe Halfway: Quantum Physics and the Entanglement of Matter and Meaning*. Durham, NC: Duke University Press.

Battiste, M. (2013). *Decolonizing Education: Nourishing the Learning Spirit*. Saskatoon, Canada: Purich Publishing.

Biancarosa, G., and Snow, C.E. (2004). *Reading Next: A Vision for Action and Research in Middle and High School Literacy: A Report from Carnegie Corporation of New York*. Washington D.C.: Alliance for Excellent Education.

Brown v. Board of Education of Topeka (1954). 347 U.S. 483, Justia Law. Accessed February 26, 2015 from https://supreme.justia.com/cases/federal/us/347/483/case.html.

Byrd, J.A. (2011). *The Transit of Empire: Indigenous Critiques of Colonialism*. Minneapolis, MN: University of Minnesota Press.

California Newsreel (2008). *Unnatural Causes: Is Inequality Making Us Sick?*

Castagno, Angelina E., and Bryan McKinley Jones Brayboy (2008). Culturally Responsive Schooling for Indigenous Youth: A Review of the Literature. *Review of Educational Research 78*(4): 941–993.

Collins, P.H. (2009). *Another Kind of Public Education: Race, Schools, the Media, and Democratic Possibilities.* Boston, MA: Beacon Press.

Crenshaw, K. (1993). Mapping the Margins: Intersectionality, Identity Politics, and Violence against Women of Color. *Stanford Law Review 43*(6): 1241–1299.

Davis, B., and D. Sumara (2009). Complexity as a Theory of Education. *TCI (Transnational Curriculum Inquiry) 5*(2): 33–44.

Derrida, J. (1973). *Speech and Phenomena, and Other Essays on Husserl's Theory of Signs.* Evanston, IL: Northwestern University Press.

Diamond, Jared M. (1999). *Guns, Germs, and Steel: The Fates of Human Societies.* New York: W.W. Norton & Company.

DuBois, W.E.B. (1898). The Study of the Negro Problems. *Annals of the American Academy of Political and Social Science 11*: 1–23.

Duckworth, Angela L., Christopher Peterson, Michael D. Matthews, and Dennis R. Kelly (2007). Grit: Perseverance and Passion for Long-Term Goals. *Journal of Personality and Social Psychology 92*(6): 1087–1101.

Geyer, Robert, and Jay Bogg (2007). *Complexity, Science and Society.* Oxford: Radcliffe Publishing.

Grande, S. (2003). Whitestream Feminism and the Colonialist Project: A Review of Contemporary Feminist Pedagogy and Praxis. *Educational Theory 53*(3): 329–346.

Grande, S. (2015). *Red Pedagogy: Native American Social and Political Thought,* 10th Anniversary edition. Rowman & Littlefield Education.

Harvey, D. (2003). *The New Imperialism.* Oxford: Oxford University Press.

Kilbourn, Brent (2006). The Qualitative Doctoral Dissertation Proposal. *Teachers College Record 108*(4): 529–576.

Ladson-Billings, G. (2006). From the Achievement Gap to the Education Debt: Understanding Achievement in US Schools. *Educational Researcher 35*(7): 3–12.

Lagemann, E.C. (2002). *An Elusive Science: The Troubling History of Education Research.* Chicago: University of Chicago Press.

Lau v. Nichols (1974). 414 U.S. 563.

Lave, Jean, and Etienne Wenger (1991). *Situated Learning: Legitimate Peripheral Participation.* Cambridge: Cambridge University Press.

Lee, S.J. (2005). *Up Against Whiteness: Race, School, and Immigrant Youth.* New York: Teachers College Press.

Lemke, J.L. (1997). Cognition, Context, and Learning: A Social Semiotic Perspective. In: D. Kirschner and J.A. Whitson (Eds.) *Situated Cognition: Social, Semiotic, and Psychological Perspectives.* Mahwah, NJ: Erlbaum, pp. 37–56.

Lomawaima, K. Tsianina, and Teresa L. McCarty (2006). *To Remain an Indian: Lessons in Democracy from a Century of Native American Education.* New York: Teachers College Press.

McQuillan, P.J. (2008). Small-School Reform Through the Lens of Complexity Theory: It's "Good to Think With." *The Teachers College Record 110*(9): 1772–1801.

Obama, B. (2009). Remarks by the President in Nominating Judge Sonia Sotomayor to the United States Supreme Court. The White House. Accessed February 26, 2015 from:www.whitehouse.gov/the-press-office/remarks-president-nominating-judge-sonia-sotomayor-united-states-supreme-court.

Peart, N.K. (2011, December 17). Why Is the NYPD after Me? *New York Times.*

Rumberger, Russell W., and Gregory J. Palardy (2005). Does Segregation Still Matter? The Impact of Student Composition on Academic Achievement in High School. Vialogues. Accessed February 26, 2015 from: https://vialogues.com/vialogues/vialogues/browse/related/8207.

Schlosser, E. (2012). *Fast Food Nation: The Dark Side of the All-American Meal.* New York: Houghton Mifflin Harcourt.

Smith, Linda Tuhiwai (2012). *Decolonizing Methodologies: Research and Indigenous Peoples.* Second Edition. London and New York: Zed Books.

Smith, Z. (2011). *Changing My Mind: Occasional Essays.* Harmondsworth: Penguin.

Sotomayor, S. (2013). *My Beloved World.* New York: Alfred A. Knopf Inc.

Tuck, E. (2009). Suspending Damage: A Letter to Communities. *Harvard Educational Review 79*(3): 409–428.

Tuck, E., and M. Guishard (2013). Scientifically Based Research and Settler Coloniality: An Ethical Framework of Decolonial Participatory Action Research. In T.M. Kress, C. Malott, and B. Porfilio (Eds.) *Challenging Status Quo Retrenchment: New Directions in Critical Qualitative Research.* Charlotte, NC: Information Age Publishing, pp. 3–27.

Tuck, E., and K. Wayne Yang (2012). Decolonization Is Not a Metaphor. *Decolonization: Indigeneity, Education & Society 1*(1). Accessed April 15, 2014 from: http://decolonization.org/index.php/des/article/view/18630.

West, C. (2003). Introduction. On *Ruminations* [CD]. New York: Welcome Rain Publishers.

Wilson, S. (2008). *Research Is Ceremony: Indigenous Research Methods.* Halifax, Canada: Fernwood Publishing.

Wolfe, P. (1999). *Settler Colonialism.* London: A&C Black.

Wynter, S. (2003). Unsettling the Coloniality of Being/Power/Truth/Freedom: Towards the Human, after Man, Its Overrepresentation – An Argument. *Centennial Review 3*(3): 257–337.

2

(DYS)FUNCTIONALITY

Educational Research and Settler Colonialism

Function: the purpose for which something is designed.
Dysfunction: [sociology] the consequence of a social practice or behavior pattern that undermines the stability of a social system.

What is the difference between a functional and a dysfunctional family? Functional families are those where the explicit purpose of the family, to provide a safe and secure context for the positive growth and development of children, is being achieved. The word, dysfunction, is used so often that its subtle but powerful nuances are lost in offhand and ubiquitous fashion. It is oversimplified to simply mean bad. To say that one is from a dysfunctional home, in quotidian parlance, is to say that the family did not reflect the image of a Norman Rockwell painting or an episode from *The Brady Bunch* or *Good Times* (insert here your popular culture reference of a happy functioning family). We hear dysfunctional and think that the needs of the family, usually more specifically the children, are not being met. However, there is more going on than simply an absence of *intended* functionality.

When parents in a dysfunctional family abuse, hurt, and hinder the emotional, social, and cognitive well-being of their children, there are still functions at play. These functions are implicit but pervasively powerful. They are often about validation, power, and insecurity. A father who strikes out verbally and physically at his children is likely serving a deep need of his own that has very little to do with his role as a father. It might be to perpetuate the ways he was unloved or mistreated. It might have to do with being more comfortable with pain than with affection. These are practices with likely long histories and entanglements, but for this discussion, the key concept here is that this behavior is dysfunctional. In these times of self-help books and lecture circuits, live your best life mantras,

Oprah-fied times, people in post-industrial societies, particularly those on the wealthier side of the scale, have become very adept at using the word "dysfunctional." In fact, the use of the term dysfunctional in middle, upper middle class, and upper class environs is tied to the ways in which this term holds lower risk for pervasive institutionalization and dispossession in society. In other words, it is leveraged in individualistic fashion, masking population-level harms that dispossessed populations experience through societal dysfunction.

However, in its ubiquity in popular culture and in some social spaces, we often lose sight of the central point that dysfunction does not simply mean bad or that there is a lack of functions in our actions and words. Rather, dysfunctional means that our explicit expressions of function do not match the implicit functions that are actually governing our actions. Put most simply, the word does not match the deed. When this mismatch occurs, the dysfunctional behavior undermines the potential of the avowed system and instead supports the maintenance of a more implicit, often damaging, structure. Educational research is, in many ways, a dysfunctional space. It is, in many instances, far afield from its avowed intention to best contribute to learning and growth, most commonly expressed through current discourses of justice. However, in its inability to disrupt the centuries-long tradition of education as the primary sorting mechanism in society, educational research must also be functioning in some way, serving some purposes outside of the avowed ones. In this chapter, I argue that educational research has served functions of settler colonialism more than it has served learning and knowledge. I analyze education research in relation to the logics of settler colonialism. To understand how educational research functions for good and ill, it will be helpful to keep dysfunctionality in mind. Having situated educational research within the overall context of coloniality in Chapter 1, I turn now to the ways that educational research is situated within the specific structure of settler colonialism. This more specific analysis is necessary to identify the ways in which these logics manifest to also better identify projects of knowledge about learning that do not emanate from settler colonial logics.

Settler Colonialism

To adequately begin an articulation of what might be a decolonial stance and praxis for educational researchers, it is necessary to understand settler colonialism, its core logics, and how they have shaped material realities and subjectivities in settler colonies like the United States. Settler colonialism, different from colonization for resources, goods, and human subjects, is based on the logic of owning land (Wolfe, 1999).

Land is the central organizing pursuit in settler colonialism, which has implications for all peoples' relationship to it. But rather than a relationship to land as ancestor, source of life, living, agentic entity, and teacher, as is often manifested in Indigenous cultures as well as African and Asian spiritual traditions

(Smith, 1999), settler colonialism seeks to acquire ownership of land by a few. As Wynter (2003) details, the larger colonial project has its genealogical roots in determining which lands were desirable, and by proxy, which beings were deemed to be human and which were not. These distinctions, with the larger project of legitimizing and delegitimizing for the sake of power, used proxies of being holier religious subjects or better subjects of the state. In the logic of settler colonialism, land is fundamentally property, and people are differentially positioned relative to their worthiness to own it. It's important to note that in this specific form of coloniality, land is relegated to resource and this then creates only certain projects of relationality among beings and land. The thirst for property and accumulation of wealth, because land is defined as a finite resource, then converts other entities into property, including people, air and sea, and status (Harris, 1993). This logic permeates settler nations such as the United States, echoing through homes, workplaces, and places of learning. As a single but pervasive example, the American Dream is often equated to owning one's own home, and implicitly, the land upon which it is built. Our relationships to the land, to each other, and to knowledge and learning, are deeply shaped by this settler colonial structure. Within education, the rationale of pursuing formal education is ubiquitously described in terms of the ability to increase one's ability to earn more money. Without a doubt, being self-sufficient is a central area of concern and undeniable material reality in capitalist societies, but to conflate learning with earning potential works from a logic that sullies what learning might organically entail, such that the learner quickly becomes a subject of the state, usually in terms of a potential kind of worker and aspiring property owner (Spring, 2008).

Through understanding the structure and goals of settler colonialism, it's possible to better identify how it is operationalized in societal spaces and projects, including educational research. This is fundamentally necessary to determine when, where, and how decolonial actions can take place. In Chapter 5, I use the example of social justice education to take up in more detail how white supremacy and colonialism shape-shift and manifest themselves even within progressive agendas when core structures are not interrogated (Spade, 2013). In what follows, though, I summarize the key tenets of settler colonialism in relation to educational research. My aim is not to fully introduce settler colonialism to the reader but to sketch it as a springboard to identifying how its logics are animated through contemporary patterns of practices in educational research. Neither is my purpose here to equivocate between violent acts of land seizure, deliberate attempts to physically eradicate Native people, and the processes of rendering humans into fungible chattel slaves. These are related and distinct components of settler coloniality. Rather than equivocate these, my goal is to be able to better identify when these logics are operating and with what material impact. It is vital to be as accurate as we can be about the epistemic frames that have shaped and continue to shape colonial trajectories particularly for projects that can operate from different epistemologies. My guiding questions in considering how and to what extent educational research animates settler colonialism have been the following:

- What kinds of logics and relationships are being created through educational research?
- What kinds of practices are legitimated?
- What are the material effects of practices that may be echoing logics of settler colonialism?

In later portions of the book, I turn to the kinds of relationality and epistemic stances possible outside of settler colonialism that I propose may help education research to better serve other logics; but to distinguish across these and better ascertain their differentials from colonialism, a more precise reckoning with the specific structure of settler colonialism is required.

First, a note about the affective associations that often are attached to education. The third guiding question, about material effects, is particularly important given the ways that education and, by association, educational research is often imbued with implicitly good intentionality, which can sometimes delay, block or render inert attention to material consequences of practices. For example, people in the United States are often critical of education broadly but much more positive about the specific local schools and teachers in their communities. Broad dissatisfaction with education is not often informed by policies, such as budgetary and zoning policies, that greatly shape educational practices (West, Chingos, and Henderson, 2012). At the same time, teachers are frequently celebrated for going "above and beyond" their contractual obligations, a discourse of dedication that keys into the good intentions (i.e., selflessness), that are assumed if one is to be a teacher. This is not to say that teachers are not routinely criticized. In fact, recent years have seen an assault on teachers, or more precisely teachers' rights to organize as a labor constituency (Kumashiro, 2012). However, this critique of teachers as a group is, in fact, more economically fueled, in line with other critiques and infringements on the right for workers to organize and collectively lobby for rights, safe and just working conditions, and equitable pay. Working from similar logics of markets and profits, a coordinated critique of teacher education programs in higher education is invested in creating fast-track, high-profit routes to certify minimally prepared teachers who quickly leave the profession. This materially works to erode the strength of unions and is enabled by ignoring extant literature that shows that the deep expertise in pedagogical content knowledge and interpersonal maturity is not teachable through rapid-fire credentialing programs. However, part of the quagmire of confronting the colonial relations that schooling has embodied more than interrupted is the endowment of "good intentions" so often ascribed to teachers. The trope of the well-intentioned teacher without substantive interrogation of the impact of practices has long obscured problematic patterns that are in need of investigation and transformation. Throughout my argument in this book, I both assume and pay little attention to good intentions. I am instead focused on impact.

Educational Research and the Logics of Settler Colonialism

The United States, in addition to many other nations such as Australia, Canada, and Israel, was founded on and maintains a project of settler colonialism (Byrd, 2011; Smith, 2011; Wolfe, 1991). Rather than a single event, settler colonialism is a continuous process and logic with three mutually dependent components, all of which work in tandem and rely on each other to maintain the overall structure.

The first component in settler colonialism is to claim the land, resources, cultural practices, and goods in a desired location. Beginning with land grabs in the 15th century and continuing through contemporary times, the United States was founded on the practice of outsiders claiming land and resources. However, in settler colonialism, there can never be enough land to satisfy the thirst of a few. This is one of the ways in which settler colonialism should be understood as a structure that mediates relationships rather than a single event. If it were a single event, such as a single invasion of land by outsiders, then settler colonialism could be more readily located historically. Rather, the logics of settler colonialism structure ongoing relationships among people and land. The physical invasions and opportunistic treaties with Native peoples echo in contemporary times with private takeover of public, potentially collective, spaces (Martusewicz, Edmondson, and Lupinacci, 2014), in the interest of accumulation of wealth. In terms of public, community-controlled spaces, this is notably felt through the dismantling of public education (Fabricant and Fine, 2012) through the proliferation of privatized venture philanthropy in education and teacher education, leveraged through educational metrics measuring teacher, school, and pupil performance (Kumashiro, 2012). As one of the last public spaces in the United States, education has experienced a surge of privatization that acts in keeping with a genealogy of land grabs. What were once public schools, with names like Washington Elementary School or Paul J. Robeson High School, are increasingly renamed and claimed for private interests, with many locations simultaneously claimed and linked through private ownership, under the names of Harlem Children's Zone, Kipp Academy, and Match (e.g., www. matcheducation.org). Au and Ferrare's (2015) network analysis reveals the small number of educational reformers who leverage disproportionately large symbolic and material sponsorship to establish private-like charters and claim those lands. In this way, we can see one of the key logics of settler colonialism, the desire for land that manifests through a logic that erases to replace. Existing public schools are replaced with privately held educational corporations.

The increasingly widespread privatization of higher education affects not just those who work in formerly public schools but also researchers who are charged with understanding how and why learning may or may not be happening within schooling spaces. As public funding for research and higher education has drastically reduced in the past few decades (Cottom, 2014), researchers from all disciplines are under increasing pressure to procure external funding (external to the university) to conduct and publish empirical research. This pressure and logic perpetuates a stance that views research and the status flowing from it as property.

Knowledge as Property

Settler–slave relationships construct and restrict relationships to knowledge. In the academy and protected through the legal system, knowledge is property. Data, publications, and even reputation, are property that are then set up to be protected for some. As Cheryl Harris detailed in her landmark legal analysis (1993), the main fulcrum through which whiteness has maintained its hegemonic hold over the figurative and material societal structure in the United States has been through property rights, with whiteness protected above all else. Harris details how, through the categorical constructs created through the law, ownership of land, reputation, and goods, has been durably protected as the province of white people, and within that demographic, most durably for men. Harris uses historical, legal, and societal analysis to illuminate the ways that property rights and white legal identities have been defined and how these rights function to protect whites' status at the top of the social order. Harris' article has become a classic of Critical Race Theory because it provides a coherent yet complex analysis of the sources of codified territoriality and the social relationships borne of stratified property rights protected for whites and inaccessible to people of color. In fact, Harris demonstrates how through the very evacuation of race-conscious codification, the law has recognized and secured land and wealth rights based in white experiences of expectation. While Harris situates these practices as in tandem with the project of a nation built from and beholden to white ownership of African slaves, this history also creates relationships to knowledge that prioritize and perpetuate settler colonialism, in which the core referent is ownership of property for a limited few.

Perhaps because land is limited when framed as a natural resource (as opposed to viewing it as an entity unto itself) or because of an orientation that generally seeks to own, settler colonialism as a structure appropriates other entities as forms of property. As Harris documents, various forms of interactions and policies work to maintain white supremacy as a form of property holding. Most relevant to the analysis here is Harris' important connection between the legal rights established in the mid-1660s to distinguish white indentured workers from African slaves, and later manifestations that have codified existing customs and social relations, including property as the expectation of rights and legal protection, traditionally protected for whites while not afforded to other racialized groups, including livelihood and credentials from higher education. As a (settler) logical flow from the instantiation of land and cultural rights, property is realized through the expectation of one's entitlement to these resources. In 2012, the United States Supreme Court heard arguments in the case of *Fisher v. The University of Texas* (2012). Abigail Fisher, a white female graduate of a Texas high school, argued that she was harmed due to the denial of her entrance to the institution because of the state's affirmative action policy, which allows race to be considered alongside other factors such as test scores, civic participation, and family legacies. That Fisher, who did not meet the state's baseline requirement of rank in her graduating class, could lodge a rights infringement court case that made its way to the Supreme Court is strong testimony itself to the expansive entitlement to property borne of a history of white supremacy established for and through settler colonialism (Patel, 2015).

Settler colonialism values ownership and property rights above all else, and it requires stratification between those who are property owners and those who aren't. Because the university-based researcher has a material status-based interest, through grants, data, and publications, the relationship to knowledge is one borne of limited resources and protectionism. Not everyone can be a settler, a landowner. Similarly, the academy and educational research has codified knowledge as ownable, but echoing Harris' central thesis, it is only property for some, namely those whose lineages are already readily visible within the culture. The vast majority of full professors in academia remain white men. Therefore, they are the predominant property holders of data and the publications coming from that data. Pursuant to the patterns of psychological bias, they are more likely to see and validate researchers who think and act like they do (Ambady and Rosenthal, 1992; Merritt, 2008). In keeping with a system predicated on differential status and competition, these property rights can be contested but are ultimately upheld for those who hold the most status in the system. Visit a graduate student discussion space online, and you are likely to see discussion boards dedicated to wondering what to do when a professor has stolen a graduate student's idea; however, it is rare for graduate students to lodge complaints through their institutions or the legal system (Slaughter, Campbell, Holleman, and Morgan, 2002). On the contrary, when intellectual property is raised with graduate students, it is more typically through a discourse of leveraging profits on behalf of the university (Villasenor, 2012), echoing the unquenchable thirst for property that is core to settler structures.

This is an apt example of how the practices of settler colonialism are dynamically imbued through material and figurative practices. Knowledge is seen as property, limited in nature, and therefore most handily pursued and protected by those who hold the most power in a stratified society (Harris, 1993). It is profoundly arguable whether knowledge is fundamentally an individual and containable entity, but the logics of settler colonialism require that some of the property be rendered more precious, with higher status, and then reserved for ownership by a few. The relationships that follow from this cauterization of knowledge animate other concerning aspects of settler colonialism. Communities and individuals, required for social science research as participants, don't have existing systems of redress if they wish to maintain "ownership" of their knowledges. It is why, for example, in their contribution to an edited volume on humanizing educational research, Tuck and Yang (2012) suggest more frequent refusals of research. In DuBoisian fashion, they switch the subject from the researcher, who often more reflects than interrupts practices of settler colonialism, to communities and peoples who stand to be researched, and within a contextual understand of the role of research in history, are at risk of being researched. Reckoning with the lived and nurtured tendrils of settler colonialism demands confronting these practices in order to change them.

In the academy, this logic of property is also vividly enacted in the framing of knowledge as intellectual property, and the "work" of public intellectuals to be knowledge producers. Settler–slave relationships construct and restrict relationships to knowledge. In the academy, and protected through the legal system, knowledge is property. Data, publications, and even reputation, are property that are then set up to be protected for some, which has potential to be converted into cultural capital and ultimately economic capital. In keeping with the logics of settler colonialism, when an entity is rendered as property, people and their rights to claim the property in question are differentially organized. For example, Institutional Review Board documents, themselves artifacts of institutions, are used to determine who "owns" the data when multiple researchers and study participants are involved. Most often, the more-senior academics take precedence in owning data, even though it might be graduate students or more-junior faculty members who have deeper and more rigorous interactions with a study's data. More disconcerting, though, is the relationship that data constructs wherein study participants do not traditionally "own" their own words or actions as they are rendered as data under the auspices of social science. What you say as a participant in a social science study, quite literally, ceases to be something over which you have sovereign domain. Even though most human subject consent forms state that participants have the right to refuse participation at any point, how many actually refuse and how their wishes are obeyed is unevenly known. In fact, across scientific experiments, participants' rights have often been secondary to the researchers' literal and figurative agendas (Harmon, 2010). And, as with any differential power dynamic, one set of rules, in this case of ownership over words and expressions, is unevenly applied. The academic and quasi-legal language of most human subject consent forms may themselves be a barrier to participants' fullest abilities to refute institutionally sanctioned research. More fundamentally though, the veritable freezing of words and observed practices attempts to suspend some things as data and other entities as data-collectors, or researchers. This does a deep disservice to the materiality and immutability of expression, verbal and not, as well as to the core nature of exchange and intersubjectivity. Through the lens of dysfunction, though, this desire for ownership of data serves the dual functions of elevating some to the position of scholar, with rights to ownership, and others as contributing goods and services to be owned.

In educational research, particularly with the growth of more intimate research stances in qualitative approaches, there has been a concerning trend of what Thomas Newkirk has called "seduction and betrayal." In a 1996 article, Newkirk examined the then fairly common language that was used in a qualitative educational research study's human subject consent form of "doing no harm." Vague language is used to describe a study's general focus but may not "tip the hat" of the researcher's more specific inquiry. Newkirk takes to task the ways that data, in this case interview and classroom observational data, is gathered and analyzed without the researchers equitably and forthrightly disclosing their thoughts about the interactions, reserving the privilege to do so in publishing the research. Since Newkirk's analysis, there has been inquiry into and destabilizing of this concept of "data," particularly in qualitative approaches. Indigenous, postcolonial, feminist, and critical methodologies have necessarily disrupted static definitions of data (Pierre, 2013; Tuck and Yang, 2014). This inquiry and pushback has productively destabilized a rigid working definition of data as said by some people (participants) in some places (the field) recorded by other people (researchers). Tuck and Yang's work, in particular, articulates the vital agency in refusing research in light of these histories.

From the durable stance of land as property and the unquenchable thirst that settler colonialism has for property in the hands of a few, it is clear that many dysfunctional relationships come into being. Along with the seizure of land and resources, though, are two adjoining components in the settler colonial project.

To sustain any land grab, the peoples already residing there must be eliminated in order for settlers to justify their seizure and the land as vacant, replacing Indigenous peoples. This is most often actualized through state-sanctioned violent erasure as a second conjoining practice of settler colonialism. As Smith (2012) put it,

> This logic holds that Indigenous peoples must disappear. In fact, they must *always* be disappearing, in order to enable non-Indigenous peoples' rightful claim to land. Through this logic of genocide, non-Native peoples then become the rightful inheritors of all that was indigenous – land, resources, indigenous spirituality, and culture.

A key trope of settler colonialism is erasing to replace. The land grabs relied on and continue to rely on codified blood quantum laws to ensure the gradual diminishment of Native peoples. This logic is present in education in the land grabs of public schooling spaces that use the law and metrics of achievement as codified strategies to claim property, specifically through the marginalizing and eroding of histories and place-based knowledges of communities (Strauss, 2014). K-12 schools are also connected to tertiary education and the forms of knowledge and knowledge production sanctioned therein. Reckoning with this relationality requires a productive destabilization of potentially facile and deterministic readings of settler colonial structures that locate some as settlers and others not, which in turn runs the danger of locating responsibility to counter coloniality for some, namely Native peoples, rather than for all.

Higher education, as a key companion pillar with the church and state in the establishment of this settler colony as a nation (Wilder, 2013), further reflects these moves of settling, including erasing to replace. The settler colonial project first constructed colleges as places for ministerial education for wealthy men, with strict focus on Greek, Latin, geometry, ancient history, logic, ethics, and rhetoric. The approach was of learning knowledge as it was presented with few discussions, or as Freire (2000) termed it, a banking approach to education wherein students, even the privileged male students allowed to enjoy this property, were seen as vessels in which the culture of the colony should be sown. For white men, though, this depositing of knowledge was with home codes and perspectives. It did not require a removal of existing epistemologies. For Indigenous communities, this banking approach erased their lived experiences to be replaced with Eurocentric epistemologies. This erase-to-replace is core to the project of settler colonialism and creates, dysfunctionally, a goal that cannot be achieved. The replacing knowledge can never actually completely fill what was erased. Colonial epistemologies can never be made home because of the dispossession it is premised upon (Anzaldúa, 1993; Asher, 2009; Battiste, 2013); the project of coloniality is antithetical to home and Indigenous knowledges. Projects of erasure are found throughout many of the historical manifestations of institutions of higher education's curricula, a logic that underlay Indian boarding schools with their self-proclaimed mission of "kill the Indian to save the man" (Pratt, 1892, p. 214). Contemporary manifestations of this logic include the maintained and protected use of Eurocentric curricula and pedagogy as common core to a solidified banking approach to higher education (Spring, 2008). Such pedagogy, for populations from nondominant cultures, explicitly seeks to erase existing knowledges and replace them with Eurocentric epistemologies and practices. For example, research into K-12 contexts that unproblematically investigates how to best and most efficiently teach academic standardized English to nonNative speakers is complicit in this erase-to-replace colonial trajectory.

The training of doctoral candidates is one of the sharpest junctures through which this logic of erasing to replace is expressed through higher education in the social sciences. In most doctoral programs, particularly those with high research profiles, one of the first rigorous exercises that students engage in is researching and writing a comprehensive literature review. The task in and of itself is one that can be used in several ways and contains within it important guidelines for engaging in any kind of research, namely searching for what others have said and done. However, along with this process, students are frequently taught, implicitly and explicitly, that they are to only cite research that has been conducted by professional academics, published in peer-reviewed publications, and that has been cited widely by other professional academics. They are also taught that academic writing should be in the third person, without references to personal experience. In those processes, apprentice scholars learn that their own experiences are to be replaced with knowledge that has been made valid as scholarship, by existing scholars. There are subtle yet important differences between honoring elders and being invested in social reproduction, and in the case of training doctoral students, the balance tips towards social reproduction. Particularly for graduate students who come from nondominant cultural backgrounds, the apprenticeship into academically sanctioned expressions of knowledge and legitimate knowledge can cause existentially and materially difficult choices and sacrifices of home codes and knowledge systems (Brayboy, 2004). The erasure of home knowledge to make way for replacement with traditionally sanctioned academic knowledge, however, is not a benign, immutable, or automatic manifestation of doctoral studies. Understanding research as enlivened by and maintaining the logics of settler colonialism helps to put these patterns into relief. As with all aspects of the settler colonial structure, it is important to keep centered the ways in which these logics have histories but also ongoing manifestations.

While the erasure of nondominant cultures is a common settler colonial logic, the fundamental investment and impulse of settler colonialism is to erase Indigenous peoples. The erasure of culture and language of minoritized peoples, works in tandem with replacing Indigenous peoples with others, such as migrant workers, but not as landowners. The logic of erasing to replace should not be equivocated as the same set of practices across all peoples and cultures. To do this actually enacts a fresh set of erasure to the erasure of Indigeneity and Native peoples' relationships to land. Sadly, though, even while discourses of equity, sustainability, and conservation abound in the Anthropocene age (Somerville, 2013), there is often a silence about the long history that many Indigenous cultures have with stewardship of land.

Within education, the erasure of Indigeneity is apparent in the knowledge production more specifically located in educational research that names white, Black, Latino, and sometimes Asian populations, but rarely Indigenous peoples, in statistics of school-based achievement. While the white center of achievement gap studies problematically reifies whiteness as normal and desirable (Leonardo, 2009), the failure to name Indigenous peoples echoes this need to erase.

Even though the recent U.S. federal policy of the No Child Left Behind Act (2001), prompted states and districts to disaggregate achievement data according to racial groups, including Indigenous students, the prevailing trope in educational research, particularly well-funded educational research, is the achievement gap between white and Asian students and Black and Latino students. This binary leverages a linked achievement rate of glossed over statistics of various Asian Americans' achievement to standards of white achievement, to fundamentally locate deficit within Black and Latino populations while also erasing Indigenous peoples. Additionally, the U.S. federal policies of NCLB and its follower, the Race to the Top Act (2013), demand identification in order to identify so-identified delinquent populations to mark them as underachieving rather than to redress a system based on colonial stratification (Leonardo, 2009). By organizing research around these policies and pursuing their funding streams, not only has federally sanctioned educational research contributed to this construction of whiteness, it has also supported the almost constant conflation between test scores and learning, an abrogation of responsibility that is fundamental to imbuing education with coloniality.

A third necessary practice of settler colonialism, and one that conjoins tightly with white supremacy in the United States, is to import slave labor in chains and render human beings as chattel. In this process, humanity is immediately put in tension with, and ultimately subjugated to, property. African slaves became chattel long before the transporting ships reached their destinations, with bodily treatment of the captured Africans becoming the first in an ongoing attempted stripping away of humanity (Spillers, 1987). Continuing through the contemporary prison industrial complex and the low-wage locations of forced migrants (Ngai, 2004), slave labor is necessary to become chattel, harvest the resources of the land and, through economic stratification and sequestering, ensure that land and property rights are reserved for a much smaller group of settlers. Higher education is, like other social fields in capitalist-anchored settler colonies, predicated on individuals holding differential status so that many are competing for the limited resources of higher status, reflected in salary and reputation (Bourdieu, 1992). Within that field, publications and grant procurement (Daza, 2012, 2013) represent the forms of capital most readily translated into higher status. By reflecting rather than interrupting hierarchies based on competition and status, the academy has sustained problematic relationships with vulnerabilized communities (Tuck, 2009). Part of this has transpired through scholarship that has worked from and validated racist premises of societal difference (Wilder, 2013) as well as the relationships between researcher and researched (Tuck and Guishard, 2013). For applied fields, such as educational research, these patterns manifest partially themselves in who is researched and what theoretical frames drive the data gathering, analysis, and implications.

A Settler Colonial Justification for Research

Educational research displays parallels and similitudes of logic to the nation's durable settler–slave–indigenous relationships through many aspects of research. One parallel is in the naming of what cultural groups are likely to be researched, racially minoritized and low-income, versus those conducting the research. Educational research, in many ways, relies on vulnerable populations to justify various foci in funding streams and publications bolstered by the potential impact in improving said vulnerable populations' conditions (Daza, 2013; Tuck, 2009). But one of the net effects of the predominance of this justificatory lens is a pathologization of particular populations that essentializes human conditions, often obscuring information that may not fit the justificatory frame of at-riskness. This is a trope that has been critiqued by scholars within and outside the field of education. Psychologist Carl Hart addressed this trend to pathologize, explaining why the field of psychology may have long-standing misperceptions about the causes and potential influences on drug addiction, "There's a skewed focus on pathology. We scientists know that we get more money if we keep telling Congress that we're solving this terrible problem. We've played a less than honorable role in the war on drugs" (Hart, as quoted in Tierney, 2013, para. 20). The role of the researcher as detector and implicit fixer or resolver of pathologies also subtly imbues the researcher with an almost omniscient-like ability to know, often, very different cultures and practices from the small population segment that makes up paid researchers (Henrich, Heine, and Norenzayan, 2010). When such frames are pervasively rewarded through grant structures and funding, and resultant publications, coloniality persists in the relation between subject and researcher.

In the field of educational research, and indeed in most applied social science fields, there is a great deal of research studying why everyone else does not achieve at the levels of economically privileged white populations. Most empirical studies close their findings with implications, and in studies of lack of achievement the most common suggestion is interventions for various populations who do not enjoy the safety, security and flourishing historically experienced by upper and middle class white settler populations. In fact, only the "at-risk," those in need of intervention, are studied. Those who benefit from preferential spots in society are not generally studied, and because of that silencing, they are re-centered as the norm. When the privileged are studied, though, it has often been from the episteme of what they've purportedly done well, to then apply such practice as an intervention to others (e.g., Duckworth, Kirby, Tsukayama, Berstein, and Ericsson, 2011), rather than from the stance of how interlocking forms of societal privilege have led to privileged social status. Meanwhile, those who are struggling are spotlighted as in need, not a system that comprehensively functions to secure and refresh higher status for those already holding power and marginalize nondominant populations.

This critique is not a new one. In the 1890s, W.E.B. DuBois was commissioned to study the "Negro problem" in Philadelphia. Instead of proceeding with the implicit damages-based frame (Tuck, 2009), DuBois reversed this pathologizing gaze and conducted a comprehensive study, the first mixed methods sociological study in the United States, of the social, cultural, and economic conditions that offered a systemic understanding of African Americans in turn of the 20th century urban Philadelphia. This stance is echoed productively in research that studies up and across liminality to, in part, shed light on colonial structures (Daza, 2006; McCarty and Lee, 2014; Nader, 1972). Despite such early and contemporary strong examples of system-focused research, the dominant approach has been to focus on the neediness of dispossessed populations. In this way, educational research utilizes deep investigation of parts in more pathologizing than liberatory ways.

This is not to say that there are not material needs that Native peoples, populations of color, and variously minoritized populations face in educational and other social settings. Rather, acritical and ahistorical educational research is complicit in the maintenance of these realities by consistently justifying its work through the lens of a presumed lack or underdevelopment leading to an achievement gap, rather than being grounded in the political, economic, and historical infrastructure of inequity (Ladson-Billings, 2006). Instead of focusing attention on the dysfunctionality required by this societal system and how else people might be in relation to each other, the trend has been to focus (pathologizing) attention on the lower strata and how to provide them with experiences that mimic those in the upper strata, echoing the pattern of erasing to replace. This desire of mimicing those in the upper strata in the hope of being integrated functions more as mythology than attainable reality. For example, the growing numbers of immigrants from non-English-speaking homes has led to a plethora of educational research studies investigating how to make these populations fluent in standard academic English as quickly and as efficiently as possible. Such studies and policies work from a tacit premise of meritocracy that, given the preferred linguistic and cultural practices, success and safety in society is available (McNamee and Miller, 2009; Patel Stevens, 2009, 2011), latent only because of the lack of these skills. This premise is fundamentally flawed as can be seen with a merely superficial understanding of the history of structural racism in formal education in the United States (Bowles and Gintis, 2011) and its efficiency to sort and segment children from differing socio-economic backgrounds. The increasingly vehement backlash against immigrant populations from the global South only serves to demonstrate the deep investment in white supremacy and the ways that structural racism permeates through various societal institutions, including education. In this way, a predominant focus on the transmission of standard academic English echoes the genealogy of settler colonialism through contemporary practices that seek to erase in order to replace with a bankrupt replacement that cannot provide access to higher status, ultimately reseating those with higher status.

Material Effects of Settler Justifications

Research Relationships and Settler Colonialism

In her "A Letter to Communities," Tuck (2009) advises communities, educators, and researchers to consider the long-term impact of communities seeing themselves through a lens of damage, as well as the implications for the viewer looking through the lens. As Tuck points out, communities often are complicit in these relationships because of a tacit, if not explicit, promise of material transformation to their conditions. Correspondingly, a researcher who is the outsider in such research relationships is engaged in his or her own construction of self, which may include aspects of being a savior, more expert, and more capable, but is undoubtedly just as dependent on the research relationship. As Jay MacLeod notes, confession-like, in the third edition of his widely read ethnography of social reproduction and racial inequity, *Ain't No Makin' It* (2008), "Sometimes I felt like a manipulative, exploitative bastard. It's not just the money. It's also the power, privilege, and prestige this book has brought me" (p. 492). In fact, MacLeod's transparency about the unseemly contours of privilege and power differentials in his research relationships is, in some ways, much more transparent in its explicitness than the sleights of hand that other researchers have used in the pursuit of data. Newkirk (1996) analyzes the seduction and betrayal involved in some qualitative research when a researcher frames the project as a minimally invasive, benign project only to then use publication space to explicitly criticize the research subjects. He notes that although people generally understand that various politics may be at play between, say, a journalist and a public official, "The subject in this case is more likely to see the solicitousness as a genuine reflection of the researcher's attitude," and then find a very different account in the researcher's publications (1996, p. 8). This relational slip of ethics is only accentuated when little opportunity exists to redress the depiction.

Of course, not all researcher–subject relationships echo this sort of unethical when opportunistic slip of representation. Subedi and Rhee's (2008) discussion of learning and unlearning among researchers and participants offers a rigor for research that is explicit on positionality and perspective. Similarly, Kaomea's (2001) work documents the ways in which knowledge that is beholden to Indigeneity and poststructural analyses must necessarily weave through the affordances of the openings in paradigms rather than operate from a single closed epistemological stance. Kaomea also addresses explicitly complex relationships with home cultures and harm within. She addresses bringing analyses to elders that draw attention to harmful messages. In this way, Kaomea interrupts facile, essentialized borders between some epistemologies as pure and others as fecund without equivocating that all knowledge is inherently equal. Through both the content of her analysis and how she engages the analysis relationally, Kaomea walks decolonial paths of knowledge as situated, complex, and mutable. The potential of these examples in this analysis of educational research and settler colonialism is not so much to offer them as alternatives or models but to query why more mainstream research is not held to these standards of explicitness in stance, mutuality, and risk.

There remains in much more of educational research, an implicit dependency of the researcher needing the participant and her "data" for the researcher's personal professional interests. Therein lies a simultaneous, although often implicit, shared investment in a theory of change in which expertise and transformation power comes from outsiders (Tuck 2009). This is an indictment also found in Fals-Borda and Rahman's (1991) call to break the monopoly of the academy, echoing Gramsci's theorization at the turn of the 20th century that all people are intellectuals but that only some are able to enjoy the societal positioning of an intellectual. Gramsci's work, though, cannot speak to contours and logics of knowledge in settler colonial societies, an important limitation for how public intellectuals, knowledge, and status are located.

Educational research in the United States and other settler nations, as an arm of state-sanctioned positioning of intellect. It profits from and is therefore dependent on the mythology of external expert as change agent. As a correlative outcropping of the positionality-specific field of qualitative studies, there has recently been more scholarship exploring the complexities of outsider statuses in research relationships. Because qualitative research posits that all truth is subjective, there has been further exploration of research methods that contend explicitly with relationships of power. Within more textured and reflexive accounts of conducting research in concert with, as opposed to on, peoples, the complexities of power and what is knowable and should be known to researchers is productively opened to questioning and negotiation (e.g., Dodson and Schmalzbauer, 2005).

The complications of positionality are no less simple for researchers who research within home communities, but there are often more-explicit discussions of positionality, responsibility, and tension within those researchers' published words (Delgado Bernal, 1998; hooks, 1999; Villenas, 1996). As outlined above, Julie Kaomea (2001) describes in nuanced detail the ways in which her identities as a Native Hawaiian and academic are in tension with each other and how, in researching within her community, she navigates a path that considers how and when to open research findings so that they may serve and be interrogated by her community rather than keep them closed out of deference to the academy's closed circuitry of publication. Tressie McMillan Cottom (2014) brings to light the ways in which presumed similarity in background leads to unexpected but meaningful conflict for her within interviewing contexts. Cottom's essay interrupts simplistic binaries of insider and outsider, in favor of a complex analysis of the ways that social locations both shift in specific moments and echo durable histories of power, status, and privilege.

These kinds of more-transparent explorations of researcher reflexivity remind us that research is always a complex set of relationships imbued, understandably, with the vicissitudes of power, conflict, interest, and contradiction that are fundamental to complex personhood (Gordon, 1997). However, mainstream, typically well-funded, educational research has yet to comprehensively, even tentatively, embrace such a view of personhood, operating still more typically from modernist and individualistic understandings of objectivity, identity (Erikson, 1959), and achievement. The predominant structure of the researcher–researched relationship reflects the logics of the settler–slave relationship where the abjectified humanity of the slave supports the solidification of the settler's higher status (Tuck and Guishard, 2013).

Understanding the logics of settler colonialism helps to situate educational research genealogically and illuminate its operating structure. In the next chapter, I take up the question of relationality of research. If we know educational research to be designed in keeping with settler colonialist purposes, what does this mean for methods and research as relational?

References

Ambady, N., and R. Rosenthal (1992). Thin Slices of Expressive Behavior as Predictors of Interpersonal Consequences: A Meta-analysis. *Psychological Bulletin 111*(2): 256.

Anzaldúa, Gloria (1993). *Borderlands/La Frontera: The New Mestizo.* New York: Aunt Lute.

Asher, N. (2009). Decolonization and Education: Locating Pedagogy and Self at the Interstices in Global Times. In: R.S. Coloma (Ed.) *Postcolonial Challenges in Education.* New York: Peter Lang, pp. 67–77.

Au, W., and J. Ferrare (Eds.) (2015). *Mapping Corporate Education Reform: Power and Policy Networks in the Neoliberal State.* New York: Routledge.

Battiste, M. (2013). *Decolonizing Education: Nourishing the Learning Spirit.* Saskatoon, Canada: Purich Publishing.

Bourdieu, Pierre (1992). *The Logic of Practice.* Palo Alto, CA: Stanford University Press.

Bowles, Samuel, and Herbert Gintis (2011). *Schooling in Capitalist America: Educational Reform and the Contradictions of Economic Life.* Reprint Edition. Chicago: Haymarket Books.

Brayboy, B.M.J. (2004). Hiding in the Ivy: American Indian Students and Visibility in Elite Educational Settings. *Harvard Educational Review 74*(2): 125–152.

Byrd, J.A. (2011). *The Transit of Empire: Indigenous Critiques of Colonialism.* Minneapolis, MN: University of Minnesota Press.

Cottom, T.M. (2014). The University and the Company Man. *Dissent 61*(2): 42–44.

Daza, S. (2006). Local Responses to Globalizing Trends: Student-Produced Materials at a Colombian Public University. *International Journal of Qualitative Studies in Education 19*(5): 553–571.

Daza, S. (2012). Complicity as Infiltration: The Im/possibilities of Research with/in NSF Engineering Grants in the Age of Neoliberal Scientism. *Qualitative Inquiry 18*(8): 773–786.

Daza, S. (2013). A Promiscuous (Feminist) Look at Grant-Science: How Colliding Imaginaries Shape the Practice of NSF Policy. *International Journal of Qualitative Studies in Education 26*(5): 580–598.

Delgado Bernal, Dolores (1998). Using a Chicana Feminist Epistemology in Educational Research. *Harvard Educational Review 68*(4): 555–582.

Dodson, L., and L. Schmalzbauer (2005). Poor Mothers and Habits of Hiding: Participatory Methods in Poverty Research. *Journal of Marriage and Family 67*(4): 949–959. http://doi.org/10.1111/j.1741-3737.2005.00186.x.

Duckworth, A.L., T.A. Kirby, E. Tsukayama, H. Berstein, and K.A. Ericsson (2011). Deliberate Practice Spells Success: Why Grittier Competitors Triumph at the National Spelling Bee. *Social Psychological and Personality Science 2*(2): 174–181. http://doi.org/10.1177/1948550610385872.

Erikson, E.H. (1959). *Identity and the Life Cycle: Selected Papers.* New York: International Universities Press.

Fabricant, N., and N. Fine (2012). *Charter Schools and the Corporate Makeover of Public Education: What's at Stake?* New York: Teachers College Press.

Fals-Borda, O., and M. A. Rahman (1991). *Action and Knowledge: Breaking the Monopoly with Participatory Action Research.* Lanham, MD: Apex Press.

Fisher v. University of Texas (2012). 570 U.S. Reports.

Freire, P. (2000). *Pedagogy of the Oppressed: 30th Anniversary Edition.* London: Bloomsbury Academic.

Gordon, A. (1997). *Ghostly Matters: Haunting and the Sociological Imagination.* Minneapolis, MN: University of Minnesota Press.

Harmon, A. (2010, 21 April). Indian Tribe Wins Fight to Limit Research of its DNA. *New York Times*, A1.

Harris, C. (1993). Whiteness as Property. *Harvard Law Review 106*(8): 1709–1795.

Henrich, J., S.J. Heine, and A. Norenzayan (2010). The Weirdest People in the World? *Behavioral and Brain Sciences 33*(2–3): 61–83.

hooks, bell (1999). *Talking Back: Thinking Feminist, Thinking Black*. Second Printing Edition. Boston, MA: South End Press.

Kaomea, J. (2001). Dilemmas of an Indigenous Academic: A Native Hawaiian Story. *Contemporary Issues in Early Childhood 2*(1): 67. http://doi.org/10.2304/ciec.2001.2.1.9.

Kumashiro, K.K. (2012). *Bad Teacher!: How Blaming Teachers Distorts the Bigger Picture*. New York: Teachers College Press.

Ladson-Billings, G. (2006). From the Achievement Gap to the Education Debt: Understanding Achievement in U.S. Schools. *Educational Researcher 35*(7): 3–12. http://doi.org/10.3102/0013189X035007003.

Leonardo, Z. (2009). *Race, Whiteness, and Education*. New York: Routledge.

McCarty, T., and T. Lee (2014). Critical Culturally Sustaining/Revitalizing Pedagogy and Indigenous Education Sovereignty. *Harvard Educational Review 84*(1): 101–124.

MacLeod, J. (2008). *Ain't No Makin' It: Aspirations and Attainment in a Low-Income Neighborhood*, Third Edition. Boulder, CO: Westview Press.

McNamee, S.J., and R.K. Miller Jr. (2009). *The Meritocracy Myth*. Second Edition. Lanham, MD: Rowman & Littlefield.

Martusewicz, R.A., J. Edmundson, and J. Lupinacci (2014). *Ecojustice Education: Toward Diverse, Democratic, and Sustainable Communities*. London: Routledge.

Merritt, D.J. (2008). Bias, the Brain, and Student Evaluations of Teaching. *St. John's Law Review 82*, 235.

Nader, Laura (1972). Up the Anthropologist: Perspectives Gained From Studying Up. Accessed March 3, 2015 from: http://eric.ed.gov/?id=ED065375.

Newkirk, T. (1996). Seduction and Betrayal in Qualitative Research. In: Peter Mortensen and Gesa Kirsch (Eds.) *Ethics and Representation in Qualitative Studies of Literacy*. Urbana, IL: National Council of Teachers of English, pp. 3–16.

Ngai, M.M. (2004). *Impossible Subjects: Illegal Aliens and the Making of Modern America*. Princeton, NJ: Princeton University Press.

No Child Left Behind Act (2001). The Elementary and Secondary Education Act (2001). Laws. Accessed March 3, 2015 from: www2.ed.gov/policy/elsec/leg/esea02/index.html.

Patel, L. (2015). Desiring Diversity and Backlash: White Property Rights in Higher Education. *The Urban Review 47*(4). http://dx.doi.org/10.1007/s11256-015-0328-7.

Patel Stevens, L. (2009). Maps to Interrupt a Pathology: Immigrant Populations and Education. *Critical Inquiry in Language Studies 6*(1–2): 1–14.

Patel Stevens, L. (2011). Literacy, Capital, and Education: A View from Immigrant Youth. *Theory Into Practice 50*(2): 133–140.

Pierre, E.A.S. (2013) The Appearance of Data. *Cultural Studies ↔ Critical Methodologies 13*(4): 223–227.

Pratt, R. H. (1892). *The Advantages of Mingling Indians with Whites*. Official Report of the Nineteenth Annual Conference of Charities and Correction, pp. 46–59.

Race to the Top Act (2013). Text of H.R. 426: (Introduced Version) GovTrack.us. Accessed March 3, 2015 from: www.govtrack.us/congress/bills/113/hr426/text.

Slaughter, S., T. Campbell, M. Holleman, and E. Morgan (2002). The "Traffic" in Graduate Students: Graduate Students as Tokens of Exchange between Academe and Industry. *Science, Technology & Human Values 27*(2): 282–312.

Smith, Linda Tuhiwai (1999). *Decolonizing Methodologies: Research and Indigenous Peoples.* London and New York: Zed Books.

Smith, Linda Tuhiwai (2012). *Decolonizing Methodologies: Research and Indigenous Peoples.* Second Edition. London and New York: Zed Books.

Smith, Z. (2011). *Changing My Mind: Occasional Essays.* Harmondsworth: Penguin.

Somerville, Margaret (2013). *Water in a Dry Land: Place-Learning through Art and Story.* New York: Routledge.

Spade, D. (2013). Intersectional Resistance and Law Reform. *Signs 38*(4): 1031–1055.

Spillers, H. (1987). Mama's Baby, Papa's Maybe: An American Grammar Book. *Diacritics* Summer: 65–81.

Spring, J. (2008). Research on Globalization and Education. *Review of Educational Research 78*(2): 330–363.

Strauss, V. (2014, April 15). Ed. School Dean: Urban School Reform Is Really About Land Development (Not Kids). Accessed from www.washingtonpost.com/blogs/ answer-sheet/wp/2013/05/28/ed-school-dean-urban-school-reform-is-really-about-land-development-not-kids.

Subedi, B., and J. Rhee (2008). Negotiating Collaboration across Differences. *Qualitative Inquiry 14*(6): 1070–1092. http://doi.org/10.1177/1077800408318420.

Tierney, J. (2013, September 16). The Rational Choices of Crack Addicts. Accessed from www.nytimes.com/2013/09/17/science/the-rational-choices-of-crack-addicts.html.

Tuck, E. (2009). Suspending Damage: A Letter to Communities. *Harvard Educational Review 79*(3): 409–428.

Tuck, E., and M. Guishard (2013). Scientifically Based Research and Settler Coloniality: An Ethical Framework of Decolonial Participatory Action Research. In: T.M. Kress, C. Malott, and B. Porfilio (Eds.) *Challenging Status Quo Retrenchment: New Directions in Critical Qualitative Research.* Charlotte, NC: Information Age Publishing, pp. 3–27.

Tuck, E., and K. Wayne Yang (2012). Decolonization Is Not a Metaphor. *Decolonization: Indigeneity, Education & Society 1*(1). Accessed from http://decolonization.org/index. php/des/article/view/18630.

Tuck, E., & K.W. Yang (2014). R-words: Refusing research. *Humanizing Research: Decolonizing Qualitative Inquiry for Youth and Communities,* 223–247.

Villasenor, J. (2012). Intellectual Property Awareness At Universities: Why Ignorance Is Not Bliss. *Forbes.* Accessed from www.forbes.com/sites/johnvillasenor/2012/11/27/ intellectual-property-awareness-at-universities-why-ignorance-is-not-bliss.

Villenas, Sofia (1996). The Colonizer/Colonized Chicana Ethnographer: Identity, Marginalization, and Co-optation in the Field. *Harvard Educational Review 66*(4): 711–731.

West, M.R., M.M. Chingos, and M. Henderson (2012). Citizen Perceptions of Government Service Quality: Evidence from Public Schools. *Quarterly Journal of Political Science 7*: 411–445.

Wilder, C.S. (2013). *Ebony and Ivy: Race, Slavery, and the Troubled History of America's Universities.* First Edition. New York: Bloomsbury Press.

Wolfe, P. (1991). On Being Woken Up: The Dreamtime in Anthropology and in Australian Settler Culture. *Comparative Studies in Society and History 33*(2): 197–224.

Wolfe, P. (1999). *Settler Colonialism.* London: A&C Black.

Wynter, S. (2003). Unsettling the Coloniality of Being/Power/Truth/Freedom: Towards the Human, after Man, Its Overrepresentation – an Argument. *Centennial Review 3*(3): 257–337.

3

RESEARCH AS RELATIONAL

Introduction

Across Chapters 1 and 2, I situated educational research in its settler colonial contexts, providing an analytic frame for understanding how and why educational research has so consistently failed to deliver on its avowed premise of ameliorating educational disparity. Given the pervasive and long-standing structure of settler colonialism, then, begs the question whether educational research is doomed to enliven these logics. In this chapter and the next, my optimistic offering is no, this is not a teleological given or *fait accompli*. Research is a fundamentally relational project—relational to ways of knowing, who can know, and to place. It has, for centuries, been situated within and animated settler colonial logics. The logics of property and ownership are undergirded by colonial needs for stratification and categorical divides but are not inherent to educational research or research writ large. While I do not suggest here that shifting referents and patterns is a simple undertaking given hundreds of years of colonial structuring, I also do not concede that the pursuit of knowledge is doomed to colonial referents. In fact, regarding research as fundamentally a relational endeavor of seeking and communicating knowledge opens up materially transformative inquiries into the coordinates used. The search and communication of knowledge is imbued with relations to social and material contexts, epistemologies, and living beings. In this chapter, I frame research as a permeable and relational force, consistently shaping and being shaped throughout the various "parts" of a research design and process. This stance productively destabilizes overly linear conceptualizations of cause, effect, objectivity, and implications while also not shirking responsibility.

Research is Relational to Contexts

That all research is situated contextually may seem somewhat obvious, given the extant literature that has described the project of research itself, from situating the origins and sociopolitical uses of the bell curve (Gould, 1996), to historical analyses of higher education (Wilder, 2013), to analyses of the ways specific nondominant populations experience higher education, the primary institutionally sanctioned location of research (Muhs, Niemann, González, Harris et al., 2012). Research is a project and product of culture, sociopolitics, and material conditions. It does not exist outside of trajectories of thought and action but firmly within. This perspective, though, stands in direct opposition to science, as commonly and historically understood in Westernized contexts, as a practice of tried and true methods that can only be undertaken by specially trained (social) scientists, and because of that special training, able to operate from and measure its worth in terms of objectivity and neutrality. These referents of objectivity and neutrality, though, are themselves far from their ideal but rather are nestled in settler logics. As Marie Battiste notes in her book on decolonizing education,

> Eurocentric science seeks principles that are universal and, as such, can be applied anywhere and any time. Born of empirical observation, made sense of by hypotheses which can, in turn, be empirically tested, Eurocentric science contradicts the faith in its knowledge. In effect, it suggests that all information is open to be disproved, thus severing it from temporal and geographic specificity. In so doing, it loses its meaning to context, and as David Suzuki has offered, such "a story … has lost its meaning, its purpose and its abilities to touch and inform."
>
> (Battiste, 2013, citing Suzuki, 1997, pp. 19, 20)

To understand research as contextually influenced and influential, though, is not to resign ourselves from being able to enter it. We do not exist in isolation from social and material contexts, separated from each other. This is true in the sense of humans being connected as well as human and nonhuman entities being connected and coming into existence with each other. This is a long-standing tenet of much of Indigenous knowledge systems. In 1995, Yupik scholar Oscar Kawagley wrote about ethnoecology, the study of humans and material environments in dynamic inter-relation, in his book, *A Yupiaq Worldview: A Pathway to Ecology and Spirit*. Kawagley's (2006 [1995]) book was, in relation to Western knowledge systems, preternatural in its discussion of ecology beyond an object/subject relation of human study and consideration, but of humans and nonhumans in dynamic relation with each other. But in relation to Indigenous knowledge systems, Kawagley's work speaks out loud a centuries-old (if not older) epistemology such that Western(ized) audiences might be able to read it, as well as exploring what this knowledge system means in an era marked not by interconnection but by the Anthropocene. In this way, Kawagley's work and how it is situated is itself an example of relationality, of ideas never being absent of thinkers in specific contexts. "Science is not an agentless juggernaut sweeping us along; there are agents in every corner of every context playing roles" (N. Drane, personal communication, March 14, 2015).

These entanglements of ideas, people, and material conditions are also one of the central areas of inquiry and analysis that Karen Barad (2007) explores in her book, *Meeting the Universe Halfway*. Barad, a quantum physicist who is also an expert in feminist social theory, explores the ways in which the meanings that we make of material conditions are intricately imbued into, through, and with those conditions and vice versa. This is particularly impactful in understanding the relationship between research and knowledge. Rather than separated as a static and isolable set of factors, phenomena are intricately bound up in attempts to measure them. In an apt example, Barad draws attention to what we know, or more so what we cannot know, scientifically about light. Measured through one set of coordinates, light is a particle; through another, a wave. According to each set's logics, the results are undeniably true, but how can two truths be accurate if they are incommensurable? Barad proposes, drawing on insights from quantum physics and critical social theory, that they are true because of the more fundamental reality that all matter and ways of knowing about matter are impermanently, continuously, and contiguously interconnected. Barad uses the term, intra-action rather than interaction, to highlight the simultaneously co-constitutive and intertwined nature of research and knowledge.

Consider this more detailed example from Barad's exploration of matter and measurement tools, themselves matter as well, specifically piezoelectric transducers, apparatuses that use electric pulses to measures shifts in surface and subsurface materials. These devices are used in a variety of industries, but Barad is focused on their medical use with pregnant women and fetuses. Piezoelectric transducers do not exist in and of themselves as might be thought, still-standing and as pure objects, lying inert in complete physical form and only slightly less inert when being used. Rather, they have been and are continually put in

> intra-action with a multitude of practices, including those that involved medical needs, design constraints (including legal, economic, biomedical, physics, and engineering ones); market factors; political issues; other R & D projects using similar materials; the educational background of the engineers and scientists designing the crystals and the workplace environment of the engineering firm or lab; particular hospital or clinic environments where the technology is used; receptivity of the medical community and the patient community to the technology; legal, economic, cultural, religious, political, and spatial constraints on their uses; positioning of patients during examination; and the nature of training of technicians and physicians who use the technology.
> (2007, p. 203)

Similarly, educational research has taken shape, continues to take shape, and will continue to take shape in dynamic relation, in intra-relation, as Barad would put it, with its sociopolitical, economic, and cultural contexts. Or more fundamentally, more radically expressed by Kawagley before Barad and articulated with his frequent co-author, Barhhardt,

> Alaska Native people have their own ways of looking at and relating to the world, the universe, and to each other. Their traditional education processes were carefully constructed around observing natural processes, adapting modes of survival, obtaining sustenance from the plant and animal world, and using natural materials to make their tools and implements. All of this was made understandable through thoughtful stories and demonstration. Indigenous views of the world and approaches to education have been brought into jeopardy with the spread of western social structures and institutionalized forms of cultural transmission.
>
> (Kawagley and Barnhardt, 1999, para. 5)

Kawagley and Barnhardt respectively articulate the differences between Indigenous and Western worldviews, and in part, they do so in order to demonstrate the ways Alaska Native peoples have, as is their history, present, and future, adapted projects of well-being and balance in the face of contradictory Western frameworks. This is not to say Native peoples have adopted these contradictory frameworks or assimilated within them. Indigenous epistemologies, as well as many Eastern and African thought traditions speak of all actions, reaction, practices, and thought being interactive. Such views demand an attention to balance and health throughout. Knowledge and practice emanating from knowledge is always in context.

Seeing all knowledge as contextual and shaping context is neither to capitulate the shape of educational research to contextual realities, such as the prominence of certain definitions of science, nor to hold it overly powerful and agentic in its own right. It is tied to and ties, binds up with humans, human history, physical objects, the planet, and the intentional and unintentional practices of all of these entities. Such an understanding is also posited in the well-known work of the philosopher Jacques Derrida, who asserted that no text or word is authoritative; they are all imbricated with traces, shadows, and referents. To date, particularly in Westernized post-industrial contexts that exhibit neocolonial logics of settler relationships, these intra-actions have shaped research to be something that has been commodified to serve the logics of property, ownership, and societal stratification.

Let's consider more, in detail, the parallels in educational research as it intra-acts with just a few of the practices that Barad lists: design constraints, market forces, and the educational background of professionals in a given area. I start with Barad's work because it speaks first, and foremost, to Western technologies. It is likely to connect most readily with Western-based readers. After the discussion, I'll return to how Barad's ideas can be read and bracketed with Kawagley's work. I include both to connect to the entry points of many readers of this text, but it is important to note that citation practices and more fundamentally, epistemic genealogies hold material force in not just our histories but our possible futures. This is a point that has been made by several critical, Indigenous and third world scholars, such as Linda Tuhiwai Smith, Eve Tuck, and Ngugi Wa Thi'ongo.

Design Constraints

Educational research has accepted design elements that render some studies more authoritative than others. There are two strong strains to this. First is the strain of objective, empirical research, with experimental, inferential quantitative designs prevailing. In many ways, the definitions of science that were solidified through this cultural space, those of reliability and validity, shaped qualitative research for many years. Qualitative research itself grew out of anthropology's methods of ethnography, an inauspicious commencement whose very design hinged on axes of researcher and the other (Somerville, 2013). Ethnography, literally meaning to write the people, from its Greek root words of *ethno* and *grapho*, fundamentally is about the study of peoples and the way they are written about. Within that entanglement, then, is the fact that someone is doing that writing and another being written about. Qualitative research for many decades embraced its particular disciplinary space of studying specific cultures (and not others) while also attempting to answer to questions of reliability (are the findings reproducible in other contexts?) and validity (do the measures capture the desired phenomena?) that had been established through concepts of research driven by neutrality and objectivity.

These concepts, though, stand in direct contradiction to an Indigenous worldview that sees all living beings and the planet in constant flux. The concepts of objectivity and immutable, isolable factors also stand in contrast to physical realities in which the actions of all beings and entities impact each other. Perhaps at no other time has this fundamental truth been so readily comprehensible. In the current Anthropocene (Somerville, 2013) era, as it's been termed, humans and their industrial technological developments have fundamentally and deleteriously impacted the planet's well-being and balance. From this understanding of the momentum of damage done in the name of universality, then, the claim of replicability, of stand-alone actions that can be measured by themselves and unhinged from the measurer, the measurement, or the specifics of place seems naive. However, this genealogy of social science has created design constraints that invoke these ideas as standards, with aberrations requiring specific justifications, often through the language of the existing standards (Wilson, 2009). Critical qualitative and critical ethnographic studies (e.g., Daza, 2009) have thoroughly critiqued such attempts to filter qualitative research through objectivist-driven concepts, which has yielded more space for research designs to draw from and produce decidedly multi-perspectival stances. The growth of postmodern and poststructural studies has also influenced educational research, particularly in qualitative, decolonial, and critical research designs. The open access academic journal, *Decolonization: Indigeneity, Education, and Society,* for example, explicitly seeks, among other formats, empirical research from qualitative designs, delineating this preference out of a decolonial dismissal of imperial notions of objectivity and generalizability (http://decolonization.org/index.php/des). Design of research, though, is just one aperture into the particular cultural, sociopolitical, and material realities that have contributed to its sanctioned versions.

Market Factors

While we may not like to consider research as being subject to economics and markets, the pursuit of knowledge in racist capitalist settler societies, particularly when coupled with career and livelihood, is intricately tied to market forces. Because education and educational research are part of a larger societal fabric, ideas and perspectives come in and out of favor and experience trends, and therefore some research projects and publications are more strongly supported, literally, through funding, and somewhat more figuratively, although still linked to economic capital, through status and reputation. Studying and writing about immigration, as I've been doing for the past several years, during this large wave of push–pull of beings across fictive nation-state borders may have more market appeal than it did in the 1970s, but at the same time, writing about the racialization processes that immigrants from the global South experience may not connect with market preferences. This dichotomy is connected to the pervasive grip of the meritocratic ideals of the American Dream that may hold much stronger sway in what consumers (the granting agency, those with status already in the system) and larger politic discourses of meritocracy demand. For example, most studies about nondominant populations are framed in such a way as to address what is often termed to be a concerning exclusion of the said populations from upward social mobility and/or the American Dream (e.g., the immigrant paradox of not being able to fully access upward social mobility after the first generation). This referent has political mettle that gives it purview and market stamina despite the historical reality that upward social mobility has only been precariously granted to specific populations, most often contingent on their abilities to shed what are seen as ethnic traditions to be accepted as U.S.-born white (Ignatiev, 2008). Perhaps because the ideologies of meritocracy and social opportunity still pervade so strongly in the U.S. as well as other settler colonies, the market for research that addresses structural racism as a given and protected feature of this settler colony has less of a broad-based market value, although there are niches where such scholarship can be found.

   In conjunction with the content and focus having more or less traction socioeconomically, the perception of specific researchers also comes into play.

Barad also mentions the educational background of the engineers and scientists designing the crystals used in the piezoelectric transducers. In terms of educational research, this can be understood in terms of the larger demographics of higher education and its historical and contemporary practices that have shaped and continue to shape these demographics. While the nation's student population is becoming increasingly diverse, the overwhelming majority of full-time faculty positions continue to be filled by white men and women (Muhs et al., 2013). From 1997 to 2007, the percentage of students of color enrolled in U.S. colleges and universities climbed from 25 to 30 percent, yet in 2007, women of color held only 7.5 percent of full-time faculty positions (Ryu, 2009). White men persist in composing the majority of tenure-track faculty positions, holding close to 90 percent of the nation's appointments to full professor (Fast Facts, 2013). While the whiteness of the American K–12 teaching force is a widely known entity (Sleeter, 2001), the whiteness of the professoriate and more specifically, the teacher education faculty nationwide is less addressed in relation to durable patterns of inequity (Gordon and Radway, 2008). However, if there is one learning that has been widely accepted from understanding race to be a strategically devised social, political, and cultural construct, it is that white supremacy affords access to intertwined sets of privileges and protection from complementary sets of social ills and dangers (Harris, 1993). This is of course not to say that white people do not experience prejudice or suffering, but that this prejudice is not institutionalized and is not subject to the craven exponentializing forces that systematically marginalize populations of color, poor populations, and nongender conforming and nonnormatively abled bodies. Whites across class, gender, and sexual identity lines experience far less physical, socio-emotional, cognitive, and spiritual violence than do their counterparts of color.

Educational researchers, of course, do not sit outside these dynamics but are as thoroughly entangled in these realities as anyone else. While extant white educational researchers may well have sharp and sophisticated intellectual analyses about racialization as a system of oppression, they still experience ongoing contexts of colonization within the protective wrap of white privilege. This may be part of the explanation of why the mythology of the American Dream and associated research frames that justify their premise from a withholding of the Dream for just some populations may continue to flourish. If one's personal experience of society has largely been a series of doors opening with new opportunities, a well-intentioned teacher, teacher educator, or researcher might seek a professional vantage to make this dream more available, perhaps more viable for other populations. It is perhaps much easier to believe in the American Dream or perhaps more palatable to use it as a frame for necessary research on those who have not succeeded within the United States. I do not mean to say that all white educational researchers hold an acritical belief in meritocracy, nor that researchers of color necessarily are more critical. In fact, no one's beliefs and epistemologies are intractable or easily essentialized with phenotype. Rather, when a concentration of an upper middle social class that has racialized protection predominates in the demographics of paid researchers, there will be population-level echoes in the ideological, methodological, and material impacts on the field of educational research (Henrich, Heine, and Norenzayan, 2010).

That this privileged population persists in control of the uppermost spaces of the academy perhaps explains why, even 30 years after the death of ethnography was proclaimed (Somerville, 2013), problematic patterns persist in white researchers pursuing and speaking of research about racially minoritized populations, to presumably white audiences. It raises questions of the larger patterns that are echoed when a young white upper middle class female ethnographer can be celebrated for her undergraduate and graduate studies of African Americans living in inner city Philadelphia.

Alice Goffman began volunteering as a tutor in a predominantly Black neighborhood in West Philly, situated next to but not integrated with the campus of the elite institution, the University of Pennsylvania, when she was an undergraduate. While she wrote about mothering in this Black community, she did not think she could add very much to the existing research literature on the topic. She did, however, see an opportunity in studying young Black men living in a police state of surveillance, control, and persecution. She became a participant observer in this culture, and her book (Goffman, 2014) provides details on the reach and contours of this police state as well as the ways that the young Black men who allowed her into their worlds, or parts of it, crafted life and vibrancy in these difficult spaces. In her work, Goffman employs the concept of fugitivity, which Keguro Macharia defines as "seeing around corners, stockpiling in crevices, knowing the un-rules, being unruly, because the rules are never enough, and not even close" (as quoted in Sharpe, 2014). In contrast to this theoretical base of fugitivity, Goffman provides her rendering of the details of these fugitive practices for the gaze and view of whites with better social status, such as herself. In many ways, how could she not do this? It is the lens through which she looks, the path upon which she walks, and the cultural context in which she, the daughter and granddaughter of well-known academic ethnographers, was socialized. To put it more simply, she comes by this honestly. But as with the example of Jared Diamond's (1999) work in Chapter 1, the point here is not Goffman as a lone researcher or unusual example but rather what the celebration of a clearly problematic text reveals about the assumptions of competence and the ability to annotate others' lives. The high-profile and positive reception of her book within academia conveys the durable comfort levels that exist for peering into cultures of color through white, even with self-avowed naive, lenses. The question is not whether Goffman does or does not offer some valuable sociological analyses of this cultural and structural space. The question is how such a perspective, one that recreates an Other and dominant culture ethnographer, receives not just unfettered passageway as institutionally sanctioned research but is celebrated, verily ushered, into academic and market prominence (Sharpe, 2014).

Goffman's work and the impact of her social location, and extant parallel examples, can be further theorized through Barad's conceptualizations of action, intra-action, and assemblage. Different than postmodern takes on knowledge being subjective, a consideration of Barad's work pushes the reader of Goffman's ethnographies to consider how her material experiences of the world, including her upbringing, and her project of ethnography, make experiences come into existence, hearable, seeable, and then scriptable within the market-based academy. However, while Barad's work speaks to the intricacies of matter and meaning, with human beings as one element, it lacks a grounding in ethics, in spirituality that is just as fundamental in shaping how matter comes into existence. Kawagley's work addresses meaning and matter as co-constitutive, as foundational to not just the nature of matter but also as investment and deference to the life of matter and life itself. In other words, understanding that the knowledge is inseparable from materiality does not necessarily move to a less colonial stance. Understanding matter, beings, and meaning as part of a broader ecology begs the question of what are more generative stances.

Parallel to the question of what research lenses are assumed preferential and competent is what work could be foregrounded instead. Public scholar activists like Ruthie Wilson Gilmore and Mariame Kaba engage, design, and facilitate direct actions and public scholarship from within and for specific communities and challenges. There are many other examples, but here I focus on the work they engage for a few specific reasons. The first is that their work is not their work alone. I provide their names in order to follow and find their resultant collective places and projects. Kaba helped to create Project NIA, the Chicago-based advocacy and popular education organization that works to end youth incarceration. Gilmore's award-winning book, *Golden Gulag* (2006), a scholarly contribution that dismantles many taken-for-granteds in understanding the growth of the prison industrial complex as a state strategy, was borne of her work with the mothers of incarcerated young people whose questions were about why incarceration had become the norm. Kaba's and Gilmore's projects share in common a resolute grasp of societal conditions, praxis that is considerate of those conditions, and ongoing practices that reach beyond critical analyses. As Gilmore puts it in the opening pages to *Golden Gulag*, "On the contrary, in scholarly research, answers are only as good as the further questions they provoke, while for activists, answers are as good as the tactics they make possible" (2006, p. 27).

All of these are entanglements of knowledge, and there is not a static identity or social location that is empirically better for researchers to have. How we engage in and with research, though, would benefit from a constant consideration of its ethnoecologies with privilege, oppression, coloniality, and for quite some time now, historical patterns of seduction and betrayal (Newkirk, 1996). How can educational research contend with being entangled with histories, currents, and do so in ways that engage futurities outside of settler colonial logics? To paraphrase from Kawagley and Barnhardt, how can knowledge be found and illuminated with a deep respect for our subsistence, not status, as dependent on future knowledge? One of many reasons why it's important to see Kawagley and other Indigenous scholars' work as foundational is that their projects of survivance (Vizenor, 2008) are simply longer and better, out of necessity and ethics.

One move toward acting on behalf of ethnoecologies is to constantly ask essential questions of any research endeavor. The first questions that I propose are in no way new ones. They are found within many nonWestern spiritual and thought traditions, as they defer to interconnections and responsibility. In Chapter 4, I take up more specifically the referents that educational research as a field should steward. Here, I provide these questions as a way to attend to relationality.

Why This? Why Me? Why Now?

Research is a relational and ontological practice. It is always entangled with specific researchers in specific spaces and with specific outcroppings. Very little of this dynamic is linearly predictable, and yet, precisely because of the variances among and within dynamics, a closer attention and rigor should be paid to questions of coordinates and ongoing responsibilities and relations among peoples, places, and practices. This stance has a long history in many worldviews and even some research traditions, such as Participatory Action Research (PAR) approaches, but by and large, is not commonplace in institutionally sanctioned research within the Western academy. As detailed in Chapter 1, most doctoral programs encourage apprentice researchers to look to the existing research literature, find a gap within that literature, and justify a research focus based on that gap. Sometimes, personal knowledge sets are germane, but generally, they are not. When introduced and mentioned, personal perspectives are often invoked in order to be "bracketed" (Tufford and Newman, 2010), that is, either set off to the side or made explicit so that the reader can ascertain the lenses through which the research is presented.

Because of the long-standing and ongoing harmful relationships between researchers working from dominant cultural backgrounds and those who are likely to be dispossessed through research that frames them as at-risk, then, researchers working in the social sciences should be attending to questions other than gaps in the literature. While we have a responsibility to understand, contribute to, and be fluent in existing research, we also are responsible for our ontological entry-points and impacts as researchers. Because all research is conducted by living beings, with specific histories, we are beholden to consider and answer, perhaps always incompletely, the three core questions of "Why me?", "Why this?", "Who now?"

Why Me?

This question should not be misconstrued as a prompt for exceptionality or destiny. In contrast to the oft-imbued message at elite institutions of higher education that further anoint already societally privileged populations (Deresiewisz, 2014), this question should prompt a humble pause and reflection on the specifics of individuals' experiences that make them appropriately able to craft, contribute, and even question knowledges. This is a necessary and ongoing set of reflexive practices that push beyond the reflexivity responses to critiques of ethnography in the 1980s. Those practices took hold in qualitative research, but have not been seen as something that all researchers should interrogate. On the contrary, views that pursue objectivity and neutrality would eschew discussions of specific entanglements of personhood, space, and materiality. And yet, all research is entangled. To deal more straightforwardly with how individuals are entangled in the research they conduct affords spaces to discuss the ways in which specific manifestations yield specific locations for the knowledge being offered. For example, educational researchers who investigate the experiences of migrant youth in schooling will present a specific set of perspectives if they themselves come from lived migrant experiences, speak more than one language, have been racialized across different nation/state/ cultural settings, and on. This is not to say that being a migrant will automatically create more useful research that addresses the experiences of migrant communities. There are simply far too many other factors and entities that are in complex inter- and intra-relation with each other to be able to parse these out in isolation from each other for the purposes of predication. But it also should raise more frequent questions about the utility of so much social science research conducted by members of the dominant culture within cultures that have been historically marginalized.

In her 2009 "A Letter to Communities," Eve Tuck advised both Indigenous communities and outsider researchers to consider the cumulative effects that come from predominant framings of marginalized communities as damaged. This holds effects both for those community members and arguably more subtly for how it positions the external researcher as a change agent, perhaps because he or she is not a member within the community. Tuck's piece has been widely cited, in part, because damage-based frames are ubiquitous through social science, and because she disrupts monolithic and unitary concepts of identity that still work from modernist frames. Central to my discussion of "Why me?" is a responsibility to consider ones' place within and among longitudinal and vast patterns of who has been researched, by whom, and from what theoretical frameworks.

For those who are insiders to communities, the contours are no less complicated but substantively different. Julie Kaomea, a Native Hawaiian scholar, wrote about the ways that she needed to approach research with both knowledge and humility, particularly when bringing to light potentially concerning practices (2001). Kaomea frames her article through a use of several theoretical stances that, at times, might seem to be contradictory, but that are also familiar for culturally marginalized groups that know incommensurate existences intimately. Kaomea then provides a glimpse into a paradox of findings and commitment to community:

I knew full well that if I chose to continue with my critique of this Hawaiian-initiated program, there would probably be many Hawaiians who had been involved in the original design and implementation of the curriculum and numerous others who are strong supporters of the program whom I might unintentionally offend.

(p. 71)

Kaomea cites Maori scholar Linda Smith's now-classic work in *Decolonizing Methodologies* (2012), and the often difficult position that Indigenous scholars are put in when faced with findings that challenge taken-for-granted or long-held community beliefs. Kaomea, in a telling move, returns to Native Hawaiian referents to determine how to share information that, while potentially painful, also holds important potential gains. She asks for forgiveness for the likely pain and contextualizes her work in the contextual necessary good that may result form the pain. In and of itself, this is a fundamentally relational act of research pursuit and sharing.

As the reader might expect, in keeping with a view that knowledge and ways of knowing are intricately tied and co-influential, there is not a static set of experiences, preferred personhoods, or social locations befitting educational research. Rather, we must be able to ask and articulate an answer to "Why me?" that is attentive to connections beyond academic qualifications and institutional affiliations. Our responsibilities should lie in how we frame, approach, and attend to the constantly fluctuating dynamics being researched and how the research is exacting impacts. These specifics, though, should be addressed, and in ways that are rigorously taken up throughout a research project and its products, not bracketed into a few introductory or concluding paragraphs.

Why This?

How we frame a research problem and its context is pivotal to understanding how it has already been understood, perhaps misunderstood, and what stances are fruitful for further understanding it.

As Barad notes, "the positioning of patients during examination," is an element that will have material intra-play with all the other elements she lists. Such is the case with anyone who is invited to be part of a social science project. They are being positioned, by the researcher, and such a positioning will have immediate and ongoing, yet not fixed ramifications for everything else in the research project and products. How Black-on-Black violence is understood, for example, through the theoretical lenses of intersectional and settler colonial theories would be subtly yet substantively different than mainstream narratives afford. Users of settler colonialism would foreground a consideration of violence among people of color in reckoning with anti-blackness (King, 2010), chattel labor for settler dominance that discriminates between respectable chattel (e.g., model minority) and criminal chattel (e.g., Black menaces, migrant as illegal) as part of conjoined projects of colonialism and imperialism (Arvin, 2013), or internal and external colonialism, as Tuck and Wayne Yang put it. Theorizing violence amid people of color through the lens of intersectionality would afford and demand an analysis of the conjoined legal and institutional categorical locations that vulnerabilize populations of color and provide articulation about how those dispossessed locations, through categorical constructs, often manifest in violence as a culturally fluid and available resource. While intersectionality does explicitly critically examine legal categories for the ways they simultaneously protect white male hetero privilege, it does not necessarily link such an analysis to land and relationships to land. Settler colonialism is insistent on this point. How a social "problem," is framed, then, even in seemingly compatible anti-oppression frameworks actually holds important differences. This insight is not a new one, particularly to beginning social scientists who have the very legitimate and frequent question of how one chooses theoretical lenses if so many address similar phenomena. Many theories can be used to explain experiences and data, but they do not do so equally.

The issue at hand, though, is that while social scientists, experienced and novice alike, may grapple with the fit and affordance of various theoretical concepts, less often are theoretical frameworks interrogated for their own social locations. In the introductory pages to his book, *Habeas Viscus*, Alex Weheliye (2014) interrogates the critical theoretical work of biopolitics from esteemed theorists Giorgio Agamben and Michel Foucault for its frequent omission of racialization processes and recurrent reinstantiation of race as empirically biological. Contrasting their work, ubiquitously popular in the social sciences, with the work of feminist theorists of blackness and anti-blackness, Sylvia Wynter and Hortense Spillers, Weheliye situates the popular yet race-muted theories of white male Europeans within a settler–Indigenous–chattel perspective.

The question "Why this?" should include the kind of analysis and consideration that Weheliye offers. He explores the content-centered consideration of what a theory affords, but also what the theory backgrounds, to what effects, and how the theory's uptake in the social sciences and citations in publications contribute materially to, in this case, settler colonial structures. Relevant questions to consider with the use of theories is what the theory affords analytically, what the theory backgrounds, to what effect, how this has played out in historical trajectories of citation and reputation, what and whose voices have been silenced, and how land and relationship to land is theorized and/or invisibilized? All of these questions are legitimate to pose to any social science research project. In the area of educational research, which I will take up more explicitly in Chapter 4, these questions are specifically located in relation to learning and knowledge (for and to the planet, humans, and nonhumans).

Why Now and Why Here?

By posing the questions "Why now?" and "Why here?", I foreground the responsibility to think about context. In their book, *Place in Research*, Tuck and

McKenzie (2015) situate all research as connected to place, meaning geographically, chronologically (but not linearly), and spatially. Attending to context, to place, to temporality, is perhaps one of the strongest ways that educational researchers can interrupt coloniality. Coloniality, with its thirst for universal truths, values placelessness, in part, because this implicitly justifies the seizure of land and the forced movement of people and resources for the interest of landowners. The fundamental colonial view of knowledge is as objective, as residing above place and space, but the terms of that objectivity cede to those who hold it, as then follows with land. Learning and knowledge are never placeless. How humans and nonhumans learn and grow is always situated in specific places, in specific dynamics.

In a mainstream magazine article, entitled, "Speaking in (Green) Tongues: Scientist Discovers New Plant Language" (Mejia, 2014) the journalist describes how Jim Westwood, a professor of pathology, physiology, and weed science, "discovered" ways that some plants communicate with each other, particularly about risks that may be coming. But these practices are not vaguely present in the same way, from any plant to any other plant. The practice is specific, and is shaped by material conditions of soil, air, water, and levels and forms of host and parasite interactions. And, the practice is not empirically new, of course, but is only new to the researcher. The article's problematic framing of discovering this language is a cue to both the colonial stance that presumes that a practice has not existed before it has been documented and analyzed by a sanctioned researcher as well as how little Western science traditions operate from assumptions of interconnectedness.

Understanding all research as being placed does not mean that we cannot know or connect across spatialities, but simply that we must be cognizant that there is not an automatic transferability to knowledge, skills, or dispositions. For example, in the popular rush to examine what has made education in Finland successful, the contrast with the United States holds important lessons, but also equally important, cautions about the distinctly different sociohistorical, cultural, and political differences across these nation-states (N. Drane, personal communication, April 17, 2015). This also means that what might be vitally important in a particular moment and place may not be so vitally important elsewhere. For example, I am an unabashed supporter of the need for more critically conscious researchers who come from nondominant backgrounds, particularly those who are Indigenous and/or racially minoritized; however, I see this as a situated need because of the long-standing deference to whiteness as intellect, capacity, and even more fundamentally, humanness. I am unequivocal about this priority, and therefore see the project of dismantling white supremacy threatened when race-neutral justifications for diversity are used, as they are most often invoked in order to deny systemic racism and support liberal humanist justifications for individuals' property holdings (Bell, 1979; Bonilla-Silva, 2009). With many of the central shifts that this book calls for, including situating research as a relational endeavor and learning as transformation (Chapter 4), there may have to be exaggerated, protective, and vigilantly self-critical engagements as we unfurl literally centuries of settler colonial logics. "Why now?/Why here?" reminds us to stay steadfast with this mantle.

What Does Research Being Relational Mean for Methods? Or Can I Still Interview People for My Dissertation?

Each fall, faculty are contacted by prospective doctoral students who are interested in furthering their education, acquiring more credentials, becoming researchers, and sometimes looking for another way of being an educator. When students call or email expressing interest, we faculty respond back, often invite them for a visit to campus, and at least where I work, there is usually one full day of mutual vetting. During the meetings I've had with prospective doctoral students, at some point in this process the student asks about my research and, then almost always, asks about potential involvement in the work. It goes something like this, "Your work sounds important/intriguing/*insert adjective that conveys interest*. If I were to come here would I be involved in that research?"

Usually I blink while thinking, "Hmmm. We just met."

It's not that I have any illusion about the strategic question of these prospective doctoral students – they should be asking about the kinds of research projects sponsored at an institution if they intend to become researchers. Nor do I operate under the illusion that research institutions are not very much about preparing paid researchers, and that does not happen very much or very effectively outside of conducting actual research. And of course I am as functionally aware as I can be of how much of a non-treat it is to work with me specifically. No, the "hmm" in my reaction is that there is no way of knowing if this person's involvement in the collaborative research I've been part of would be beneficial to the people involved outside of the university. Research is a fundamentally relational, cultural, and political practice. As an intentionally community-involved, collaborative researcher, such a question without contextual knowledge leaves me at a complete loss. I shouldn't be able to answer that question, as it is simply not up to me completely, and relationships for a newcomer have to be built all around, not just with the person who holds the institutional designation of principal investigator.

When we engage in many academic research activities, though, there tends to be a generic, tacit reference to accepted graduate students (and more so faculty for that matter) as inherently, perhaps unilaterally, capable of conducting research. For example, in applying for and procuring grants, an essential activity for any faculty member at a research institution, it is wise to include line items to fund graduate students, to both people the work of the research as well as to support their stipends, tuition needs, and their development as researchers. But here's the problem: acceptance into a graduate program does not necessarily tell us very much about the ability to be of service to a specific population in specific contexts working on often multi-faceted, hydra-headed issues (Picower and Mayorga, 2015) of equity and oppression. Considering the demographics of those who make it into doctoral programs at research-intensive universities, the viability of that population knowing the needs, logics, and intelligences in communities far flung from the academy should minimally be up for discussion. Of course, neither do the initials P, h, and D necessarily tell a person, particularly one not intimately familiar with the academy, anything about those capacities. In fact, those initials have far too often meant seduction, betrayal, and opportunism. It is for these good reasons that so many communities have enacted their own processes (Indigenous Rights Radio, 2014) of ascertaining how and when to grant external researchers entry. In fact, while it has become the bane of some researchers' existences, the practice of several Indian nations, school districts (e.g., Navajo Human Research Board, 2007), and other collectives to have minimally named their own research clearance procedures and sometimes barred external researchers should be seen as a powerful act of empowerment and refusal (Tuck and Wayne Yang, 2014) in the face of so much appropriation.

Working across the very different and sometimes oppositional needs of marginalized communities and university-based researchers should not be, as it has often been, a question of how the researcher can "gain access." In participatory approaches to research, for example, access itself is an insufficient if not problematic concept. Most participatory approaches to research are long-term and multi-perspectival and as such, access is neither a single point of entry nor singly conferred. It takes a long time to establish trust, to build relationships, to engage in ongoing, messy dialogues and practices that interact with systemic issues, which are, by definition and reality, never a single-fulcrum issue. To put this in terms used by Barad and Somerville, they are entanglements. None of that, though, is well reflected in traditional linear research designs of problem, literature review (from the academic library), methods, findings, and results.

This, however, does not mean that tactics like observation, watching, interviewing, and mapping, to name the methods most frequently found in qualitative designs, are no longer viable. The tension arises when such methods are used in a fashion that mimics a desire for the mythological objectivity most frequently claimed through inferential statistical designs. It is more than possible and exists in extant examples, to devise and roll out qualitative research projects involving interviewing, observing, and coding. The questions and approaches that control for variables are important, but for different questions than those that tend to be asked and pursued by marginalized communities finding ways to survive despite what a heteropatriarchal racist settler state might have in mind for them. Life just isn't that controllable outside of labs. It's much messier, and it should be. The mess also yields insights, if we can shake off the logarithms of the academic processes long enough to see them.

For example, in a collaboration with a group of youth, educators, and social justice activists living in the same city, I was working with two graduate students to investigate the contours of settings outside of school that support critical consciousness of youth. In this mix, sometimes some of the youth have sophisticated analyses about a just society, and sometimes not, as would be the case with any group. At one meeting, there were some strongly misogynistic phrases thrown around at the end of one of our sessions. Now, adherence to the previously designated inquiry into social justice development might mean asking some of the youth to participate at a later date because their comments and practices do not resonate with any descriptor of social justice praxis and therefore would yield little in the way of data. In such a scenario, the graduate students might interview those who remained in the program and conduct some activities with them, but they wouldn't necessarily be directly making central decisions about who should remain in the program, as those decisions would be for the principal investigator, not the apprentice graduate students. But in this approach, insight from the graduate students was crucial to making meaning of the interactions. They had been onsite, working as long-term substitutes with these youth and therefore, could pose plausible theories to make meaning of the comments within a larger knowledge base of these youth, and provide suggestions on how to proceed. These "students" have that place as researchers because of their time in the school, certainly, but that would not have come to be without their ability into those roles in the school, be effective teachers of the youth, and to be critically reflective practitioners. It also helps that they understand aspects of navigating the world from nondominant social locations through their own lived experiences. In such embedded and complex projects of knowledge pursuit, it is my hope that these graduate students are learning something much more important than a textbook-worthy semi-structured interview protocol. I'm hoping they're learning that if the research is worth its mettle, it won't simply seek the cherries in the data that all but shout "quotable," but that the research makes the theories work as well as works the theories in relation to the data. That is research that is considerate of its fundamental nature of movement and impact without trying to control every aspect.

Which brings me back to the blinking I do when asked if someone I just met three minutes ago would be able to work, to be of service, to be a "researcher" in such a setting. I've yet to arrive at a better, more honest answer than "Let's see how it goes" because that contains my desire to delay making promises that serve academic processes but at the backgrounding of other participants.

Does Answerability Mean that Everyone Should Be Doing Participatory Action Research or Qualitative Research?

No. While we have a long and vast history of imperialist-infused prominence of protecting stakes in objectivity and neutrality, social science and educational research more specifically should not lurch to uniformly adopting a different particular epistemic stance, methodology, or approach, particularly while so few are fluent with the echoes and ongoing structure of settler colonialism. Decolonization requires, at minimum, a consideration of how ideologies impact material practices, how practices are always epistemically shaped, and vice versa.

To swap, then, a set of material practices for another flirts with cosmetic changes that may do precious little to interrupt material coloniality. In the greater Mikmaq and Wamponoag lands, more commonly known as Boston, there are now over 60 institutions of higher education. Of those, about a dozen have doctoral programs in educational research. Imagine if just half of those doctoral programs began requiring their students to use participatory approaches with "the community." Of immediate concern is the need to better consider who and what counts as "the community," and how that nominal does work to also name and locate higher education and research as beyond the community. But more central to my point here is that schools, community-based organizations, families, and spaces would be quickly inundated. Already poorly compensated nonprofit workers, who are strapped for fiscal, human, and material resources, would be in the unenviable position of hosting graduate students and paid researchers who may be helpful but also would require training to learn some of the institutional history, of the nonprofit organizations. Worse yet, they might ride roughshod over the cultural specifics of the nonprofit organization's population's needs. What happens in the spaces where the needs of the nonprofit organization are incommensurable with the needs of the institutionally affiliated personnel, such as university institutional review board clearances, timelines for graduation, and captured data? What happens when, as more and more higher education moves from public funding sources to short-term private sources, the grant runs out?

For example, in some of my work with undocumented youth (Patel, 2013), the university-based procedures for informed consent ran counter to the participatory and activist goals that we had as a collective. Typically in science, and particularly within qualitative studies, masking the identities of participants is seen to be one of the pre-eminent ways to protect participants. One of the projects I've been involved with sought to interrupt narratives of meritocracy as they are applied to undocumented migrants. In this project, undocumented youth activists used their names and their stories in loud and explicit ways as forms of public pedagogy, activism, and social agitation. None of them wanted their names masked in the research. To them, this seemed to be completely out of keeping with what they were trying to counter: an anonymizing of identity to deny personhood. To conduct research with them into these practices begged at minimum a reconsideration of what is seen to be default "good practice" in university-sanctioned research. For a more thorough discussion of the social, political, economic, and cultural locations of consent in university research, see Tuck and Guishard (2013).

Does Prioritizing Holism and Intra-Relationships Mean That It's Incorrect to Look Closely at Specifics?

One of the great draws and strengths of advanced higher education is the ability to focus in closely on a topic and/or particular methodologies. To become expert in a field requires depth in the field and an automaticity with its particular schematics. However, one of the drawbacks of this rigor of study is a segmented and isolated set of expertises. While there is not anything inherently wrong with depth and expertise, it becomes problematic when expertise sets are incapable of speaking to each other and lose a sense of how multiple forces interact in everyday lives. For example, in the late 1980s and early 1990s, several studies indicated that there is an extremely strong correlation between lead levels and occurrence of violent crime in cities. However, these compelling results were not taken up or even pursued by criminologists. As Drum explores in his 2013 article about the general shrug that this compelling finding received, part of the answer to why this has not been taken up has to do with how specializations tend to privilege certain types of explanations, and background others. He quotes public policy professor Mark Kleiman, who has studied promising methods of controlling crime. Kleinman stated that because criminologists are sociologists, they are more drawn to sociological explanations, not medical ones. Without a doubt, all disciplines are susceptible to this kind of patterned meaning making. The problem, therefore, is not in deep knowledge, but in siloed knowledge that rarely has the opportunity to be filtered and connected through a different lens. This is a particularly robust place for educational research to show deeply needed research. Educational research is not a discipline unto itself. It is a geographic space in society. To understand it, economists, sociologist, linguists, anthropologists, historians, and psychologists could all contribute perspectives. As a field, though, educational research should draw from and work across those disciplines, having each be essential and simultaneously insufficient on its own.

Conclusion – Educational Research as Relation

Education and educational research have always been entangled with intra-acting with material conditions of children, teachers, families, communities, and the planet. However, this stance of seeing research relationally, inextricably bound in its material contexts, has not been commonly taken up. Perhaps this is because of an echoing default to and desire for an objective or removed position of research and therefore researchers. However, to be so, educational research would have to be an overwhelmingly unique and spontaneous generator of decontextualized phenomena. Clearly, this is not the case. What would it mean, then, for educational research to be more explicit about how it is situated within, affecting, and affected by other material conditions and ideologies?

Headlines bring the frequent newest case of legal and extralegel violence against people from non-dominant communities, but rarely is it asked how research is part of this history and contemporary structure. In the summer of 2013, George Zimmerman, a white self-appointed neighborhood watchperson, was acquitted of legal charges stemming from his arrest after shooting and killing unarmed Trayvon Martin, a young black male who was out for a walk. For populations of color, the murder and subsequent acquittal were testimony to the engrained structural racism endemic to the United States. Around the same time as the acquittal, educational researchers in the United States, as well as other locations, were nearing the deadline to submit proposals to the largest convening of educational researchers in the continent, the American Educational Research Association. I wrote the following short essay out of sheer frustration at seeing a disconnect between so many conference proposals, manuscripts, and the societal context in which they take place. It seems an appropriate summation of what it means to see educational research as relational and then seek realistic coordinates from a place of integrity.

WHAT DOES THE TRAYVON MARTIN CASE HAVE TO DO WITH EDUCATIONAL RESEARCH?

I write this still reeling from the Zimmerman verdict that verified, again, that the infrastructure of this nation is one built to support and maintain white supremacy. My social media feeds are flooded by the posts of pain, anger, and resentment that people of color are feeling as they are reminded of the core truths about this nation. Many of my educational researcher colleagues are also likely preparing their proposals this week to present at the American Educational Research Association that takes place every spring.

What does one have to do with the other? Everything. Schooling is one of the key locations of social reproduction in society. That means, put less academically, that schools are one of the core spaces where some are privileged and others are marginalized. It is where standards of competency and images of intellect are conveyed, all culturally based and typically, biased. Schools, as a part of a nation built on white supremacy, reflect this culture. From pedagogy and curriculum to policy and private interests, schools do the bidding of a nation constructed to eradicate Indigenous populations, ensure that populations of color are trained to populate low-income home, work, and incarceration spaces, and maintain property rights for European Americans.

Educational research undoubtedly figures into this equation and therefore we must ask what our research does to advance, topple, or create alternatives outside of this deliberate design of domination. As we prepare our proposals and proofread the required sections of theoretical framework, research methodology, and significance, let us do so with some modicum of answerability to the ways in which schooling has acted, for centuries, to name Indigenous peoples as savage to treat them savagely, African American people as thugs to treat them thuggishly, and immigrant populations as peripheral to place them on the side. Higher education and the research industrial complex are a fundamental part of this landscape and calculus of schooling.

The proposals that we prepare should minimally explicitly address how the research we present addresses a system that requires individualistic ideas of meritocracy to maintain a white heteropatriarchal supremacy. Meritocracy tells us that if we work hard, play by the rules, and are good people, this system will reward us. Put in terms of higher education, this is the logic used to position publications in high status journals as the sure route to promotion and tenure. Put in terms of K-12 schooling, it comes down to the grades and, increasingly, test scores.

So, for AERA, if the research is about increasing those beloved test scores, at least be explicit about what Eve Tuck implores social science to do and address your theory of change: how exactly will the better scores alter the "open season on black boys" as Gary Younge put it so eloquently? A bit more broadly construed, how might this research help different populations locate their social advantage and act responsibly from those places? I don't imagine educational research to be able to speak to the triage needs that many of us are feeling right now, but neither should it require six steps of extrapolation to address explicitly systems of codified colonialism, racism, and patriarchy.

Educators and educational researchers often work from the theory that with a good education, social mobility and achievement and safety is likely in the United States. Trayvon Martin was an honor student with a 3.7 GPA and had a full-ride scholarship to a college. He played by those oh-so-precious rules of meritocracy, but Zimmerman played by the much more fundamental rules of white supremacy and violence.

This essay has within it initial, incomplete but necessary stances to engaging research as answerable to not just "larger" societal problems but as having played a role in coloniality for hundreds of years. However, this is not a commonly shared or rigorously understood history. Because of that, there have been, and we should expect that there will continue to be, ways that educational research is connected to contexts in less than helpful ways. Attending to our role within shifting contexts, our own shifting roles, in a constant state of flux with each other is, at the onset, a seemingly daunting task, particularly when we understand the premise that there cannot be a pure knowability of any phenomenon, educational or otherwise. However, this stance also affords the opportunity to unfurl the grip on control and instead situate ourselves as answerable. While this is a preferable stance for anyone, particularly given the historical stance of ownership and territory that is fundamental to settler colonial logics, as educational researchers we are also able/obligated to be specific about what we are answerable to. In the next chapter, I discuss three key tenets that educational research should be answerable to: learning as transformation, knowledge as impermanent, and genealogies of coloniality.

References

Arvin, M.R. (2013). *Pacifically Possessed: Scientific Production and Native Hawaiian Critique of the "Almost White" Polynesian Race*, PhD dissertation, University of California, San Diego.

Barad, Karen (2007). *Meeting the Universe Halfway: Quantum Physics and the Entanglement of Matter and Meaning*. Durham, NC: Duke University Press.

Battiste, M. (2013). *Decolonizing Education: Nourishing the Learning Spirit*. Saskatoon, Canada: Purich Publishing.

Bell Jr, D.A. (1979). *Brown v. Board of Education* and the Interest–Convergence Dilemma. *Harvard Law Review 93*, 518.

Bonilla-Silva, E. (2009). *Racism without Racists: Color-blind Racism and the Persistence of Racial Inequality in America*. Third Edition. Lanham, MD: Rowman & Littlefield.

Daza, S. (2009). The Non-Innocence of Recognition: Subjects and Agency in Education. In: R.S. Coloma (Ed.) *The Postcolonial Challenge in Education*. New York: Peter Lang, pp. 326–343.

Deresiewicz, William (2014). *Excellent Sheep: The Miseducation of the American Elite and the Way to a Meaningful Life*. New York: Free Press.

Diamond, Jared M. (1999). *Guns, Germs, and Steel: The Fates of Human Societies*. New York: W.W. Norton & Company.

Drum, Kevin (2013). America's Real Criminal Element: Lead. *Mother Jones*. Accessed November 4, 2014 from: www.motherjones.com/environment/2013/01/lead-crime-link-gasoline.

Fast Facts: Race Ethnicity of College Professors (2013). National Center for Educational Statistics. Accessed September 9, 2015 from: https://nces.ed.gov/fastfacts/display.asp?id=61.

Gilmore, R.W. (2006). *Golden Gulag: Prisons, Surplus, Crisis, and Opposition in Globalizing California* (Vol. 21). Berkeley, CA: University of California Press.

Goffman, Alice (2014). *On the Run: Fugitive Life in an American City*. Chicago: University of Chicago Press.

Gordon, A.F., and J. Radway (2008). *Ghostly Matters: Haunting and the Sociological Imagination*. Second Edition. Minneapolis, MN: University of Minnesota Press.

Gould, Stephen Jay (1996). *The Mismeasure of Man*. Revised and expanded Edition. New York: W.W. Norton & Company.

Gutiérrez y Muhs, G., Niemann, Y.F., Gonzalez, C.G., and Harris, A.P. (2012). *Presumed Incompetent: The Intersections of Race and Class for Women in Accademia*. Utah State University Press.

Harris, C. (1993). Whiteness as Property. *Harvard Law Review 106*(8): 1709–1795.

Henrich, J., Heine, S.J., and Norenzayan, A. (2010). The Weirdest People in the World? *Behavioral and Brain Sciences 33*(2–3): 61–83.

Ignatiev, Noel (2008). *How the Irish Became White*. First Edition. New York: Routledge.

Indigenous Rights Radio (2014). Accessed September 7, 2015 from: http://consent.culturalsurvival.org/radio-spots-search/field_category/International%20Human%20Rights%20Mechanisms-9/language/en.

Kaomea, J. (2001). Dilemmas of an Indigenous Academic: A Native Hawaiian story. *Contemporary Issues in Early Childhood 2*(1): 67. http://doi.org/10.2304/ciec.2001.2.1.9.

Kawagley, Angayuqaq Oscar (2006) [1995]. *A Yupiaq Worldview: A Pathway to Ecology and Spirit*. Second Edition. Long Grove, IL: Waveland Pr. Inc.

Kawagley, A.O., and R. Barnhardt (1999). Education Indigenous to Place: Western Science Meets Native Reality. In: Gregory Smith and Dilafruz Williams (Eds.) *Ecological Education in Action*. New York: State University of New York Press, pp. 117–140.

King, T.L. (2010). One Strike Evictions, State Space and the Production of Abject Black Female Bodies. *Critical Sociology 36*(1): 45–64.

Mejia, D. (2014). Speaking in (Green) Tongues: Scientist Discovers New Plant Language. *Newsweek.* Accessed November 4, 2014 from: www.newsweek.com/speaking-green-tongues-scientist-discovers-new-plant-language-264734.

Muhs, G.G. y, Y.F. Niemann, C.G. González, A.P. Harris et al. (2012). *Presumed Incompetent: The Intersections of Race and Class for Women in Academia.* First Edition. Boulder, CO: Utah State University Press.

Navajo Human Research Review Board (2007). *IRB Research Protocol Application Guidelines.* Navajo Division of Health.

Newkirk, T. (1996). Seduction and Betrayal in Qualitative Research. In: Peter Mortensen and Gesa Kirsch (Eds.) *Ethics and Representation in Qualitative Studies of Literacy.* Urbana, IL: National Council of Teachers of English, pp. 3–16.

Patel, L. (2013). *Youth Held at the Border: Immigration, Education, and the Politics of Inclusion.* New York: Teachers College Press.

Picower, B., and E. Mayorga (Eds.) (2015). *What's Race Got to Do With It?: How Current School Reform Policy Maintains Racial and Economic Inequality.* New York: Peter Lang.

Ryu, M. (2009). *Twenty-Third Status Report: Minorities in Higher Education. 2009 Supplement.* Accessed from: www.zotero.org/leighpatel/items/action/newItem/collectionKey/JXFDIK3F/itemType/report/mode/edit.

Sharpe, Christina (2014). Black Life, Annotated. *The New Inquiry.* Accessed November 4, 2014 from: http://thenewinquiry.com/essays/black-life-annotated.

Sleeter, Christine E. (2001). Preparing Teachers for Culturally Diverse Schools Research and the Overwhelming Presence of Whiteness. *Journal of Teacher Education 52*(2): 94–106.

Smith, Linda Tuhiwai (2012). *Decolonizing Methodologies: Research and Indigenous Peoples.* Second Edition. London and New York: Zed Books.

Somerville, Margaret (2013). *Water in a Dry Land: Place-Learning through Art and Story.* New York: Routledge.

Tuck, Eve (2009). Suspending Damage: A Letter to Communities. *Harvard Educational Review 79*(3): 409–428.

Tuck, Eve, and M. Guishard (2013). Challenging Epistemological Authority in Qualitative Research: An Emancipatory Approach. In: Tricia M. Kress, Curry Malott, and Brad Porfilio (Eds.) *Challenging Status Quo Retrenchment: New Directions in Critical Qualitative Research.* Charlotte, NC: Information Age Publishing, pp. 3–27.

Tuck, Eve, and M. McKenzie (2015). *Place in Research: Theory, Methodology, and Methods.* New York: Routledge.

Tuck, Eve, and K. Wayne Yang (2014). Unbecoming Claims: Pedagogies of Refusal in Qualitative Research. *Qualitative Inquiry 20*(6): 811–818.

Tufford, Lea, and Peter Newman (2010). Bracketing in Qualitative Research. *Qualitative Social Work 11*(1): 80–96.

Vizenor, G. (Ed.) (2008). *Survivance: Narratives of Native Presence.* Lincoln, NE: University of Nebraska Press.

Weheliye, A.G. (2014). *Habeas Viscus: Racializing Assemblages, Biopolitics, and Black Feminist Theories of the Human.* Durham, NC: Duke University Press.

Wilder, C.S. (2013). *Ebony and Ivy: Race, Slavery, and the Troubled History of America's Universities.* First Edition. New York: Bloomsbury Press.

Wilson, S. (2009). *Research Is Ceremony: Indigenous Research Methods.* Black Point, NS: Fernwood Publishing Co., Ltd.

4
ANSWERABILITY

Over the course of the first three chapters, I have addressed and situated the ways that educational research is imbued with the logics and ideological structures of settler colonialism, with material effects for learning, learners, and research. In this chapter, I turn to what referents are possible beyond and instead of ownership and property. One of the challenges of decolonial work is contending with the ways that coloniality functions in both the aggregate and specific. The coordinates and shapes of how coloniality is occurring are also pivotal in engaging in decolonial praxis. Here, I suggest that it is possible to shift coordinates from property acquisition to being answerable for learning, knowledge, and context.

As I was about to graduate with my doctorate in education, I experienced consistent ambivalence about the academy. When I was offered a policy position working in the state education department of Hawai'i, I grabbed at the chance to interact with education as a policymaker, in some ways, to further my inquiry into schooling as a system, but from the vantage of a policymaker. In my role, I was in charge of literacy professional development for all teachers in the state. This role was intensified because of a federal court order for the state's schools to substantively improve literacy learning for all students.

When I arrived to begin the position, the state was already in default of this order. While under justified pressure from the federal government and court system, I took up outrigger paddling as a counterbalance. Twice during the week, and every Saturday, I met my teammates, and we practiced paddling, learning how to function as a collective. In every move, the goal was to be coordinated with each other. I learned how to watch my teammates for their movements, with an ear open to the anchor and her rhythm. I learned to adjust the pace, force, and pitch of my paddle, but only in relation to the movement around me, and the constantly changing conditions of the water and air. I learned, by experience and through mostly silent mentoring, how to be with the earth and ocean as a guest to its powers. For the most part, when I wasn't on that canoe, I was working, traveling to all the islands each week, building with teachers and administrators, strategizing with elders on the weekends, learning about the ongoing legacy of neocolonial education in Hawai'i, and trying to alter that path through multiple forms of critical literacy education.

In hindsight, outrigger paddling taught me more about my place in Hawai'i than could any single person or set of experiences, and it enabled me to be a better policymaker while still a stranger and guest. What I learned from outrigger paddling was triple-fold and is relevant for this discussion of learning and coloniality: coordinates are constantly shifting, we are all part of a larger collective of complex forces, and there is, at best, a thin slice of what we can absolutely control at any moment. As much as it may seem that there are certain referents, whether it is the location of Mount Haleakala to a paddler or the designation of African American for a researcher, coordinates are always shifting. This may seem contrary, as objects, places, and even people are often discussed as stable; e.g., a pen is a pen, that mountain's height is 6,780 meters, and I am a South Asian woman. But as noted in Indigenous epistemologies and with different notes in Western quantum physics, nothing is completely fixed; far from it. The topography of a particular location on Mount Haleakala is shifting, just like a person's identity, or more accurately put, subjectivity is also unfixed. While there are relatively durable qualities that may be constituted consistently, these are not absolute; they do not exist independently or universally. They come into existence through relation to other entities, and therefore, that coming into being is subject to conditions, which because of their requisite impermanence are also unfixed. This makes controlling for factors, predicting outcomes, scaling up, all ubiquitous in research terminology, much more elusive than might appear. It doesn't mean that we don't act, but that to act out of a view of universal truth for all living beings is irresponsible and, not unrelatedly, an anchor of coloniality. As Huey P. Newton once said, power is the ability to define phenomena and make them act in a desired manner, such as naming someone else's condition (fixedly), and have them believe it. These lessons are important precursors to keep in mind in moving away from a settler colonial set of referents and recalibrating educational research's responsibilities (Battiste, 2013). Settler colonialism trains people to see each other, the land, and knowledge as property, to be in constant insatiable competition for limited resources. From the vantage of the settler, the focus becomes maintaining and growing those property rights. All others are positioned in relative locations around that center, being erased from visibility or supporting the settler center while antithetically never being able to achieve its status. Social science research has grown a disconcerting synchrony with this worldview, pursuing knowledge as something to be owned, in the interest of it being rewarded with status and capital. Such a stance can quickly collapse complicated projects of social change into agendas of assimilation, with little regard for the deleterious effects of its teleology. However, the ways in which research has echoed, been situated with and situated itself in, settler colonial logics is also the place where options exist for shifts. It is possible to answer to a different set of ethical coordinates than settler colonialism. In fact, research being at its core a project of knowledge, is more accurately understood as entities that are not wholly individualist and ownable projects.

Several questions arise immediately in any kind of anticolonial or decolonial project, but perhaps first is what, if not ownership, property, and dominion, should be the purpose of educational research? I propose that educational research should be answerable to the referents of learning, knowledge as ontological, and context. By staying steadfast to answering, to being answerable to those coordinates, I suggest that educational research can manifest a praxis of ethics and move away from a praxis of coloniality.

Answerability

In her careful 2013 analysis of decolonizing education, Marie Battiste suggests 'response-ability' to move beyond discourse and language to practice and action. At its heart, the concept of accountability could have held similar strains but has been so thoroughly co-opted by neoliberal projects of imperialism and social control that it is has become all but synonymous with draconian top-down strategies that seek to measure in order to sanction and surveille. Maori scholar Linda Tuhiwai Smith (2012), in her classic yet still ground-breaking book, *Decolonizing Methodologies*, outlines several principles that decolonial methods feature, including research that emanates from and prioritizes Indigenous peoples' sovereignty. With deference to these important works, I suggest answerability as a construct and cognitive tool that can help educational researchers articulate explicitly how their work speaks to, with, and against other entities. Often, the challenge in learning about coloniality is a sense of paralysis in the face of its expansive reach and history, and yet, that ubiquity also offers opportunity. Because coloniality has been so pervasive, we can think about how our actions, our research agendas, the knowledge we contribute, can undo coloniality and create spaces for ways of being in relation that are not about individualism, ranking, and status. Answerability includes aspects of being responsible, accountable, and being part of an exchange. It is a concept that can help to maintain the coming-into-being with, being in conversation with.

As Bakhtin (1986) theorized, our ideas, our words, have all been said before:

> Every utterance must be regarded as primarily a *response* to preceding utterances of the given sphere (we understand the word "response" here in the broadest sense). Each utterance refutes, affirms, supplements, and relies upon the others, presupposes them to be known, and somehow takes them into account … Therefore, each kind of utterance is filled with various

kinds of responsive reactions to other utterances of the given sphere of speech communication.

(p. 91)

Bakhtin meant *response* not only in the literal sense of what was just uttered before but in a much farther-reaching sense, including beings near and far in myriad contexts. Responses involve speakers and listeners. This speaks not only to the nature of knowledge, which I will return to later in this chapter, but also to the potential of stances that educational researchers can assume as they turn away from ownership and coloniality.

There is an answerability in the roles we have with each other. How we interact is not just about that specific moment and context but echoes across contexts. It is always connected to figurations that have come before but do not statically predict what can transpire. In other words, matter, energy, and information exchanges and transformations in the prediscursive materially realize the social semiotic but are not reducible to it (Barad, 2007).

This element of the prediscursive is related to poststructural feminist theorizations of subjectivity (e.g., Ahmed, 2006; Grosz, 1994), in that the ways that we come into being in space and time, how we carry ourselves and act, are dynamic mixtures of affordances that have been shaped by and echo long-standing yet not sealed histories (Baldwin, 1963; Gordon, 1997). Theorists who have addressed materiality (Barad, 2007; Kawagley, 2006 [1995]), contend that subjectivities are never removed from material conditions, that those becomings enact and exact material consequences. Our social locations and histories have an impact on not just what we say but how we say it, and what meanings are made of our utterances. Considering educational research's role in the perpetuation of settler–slave–Indigenous relationships, those of us employed as educational researchers are answerable to these deep trajectories. Given these deep trajectories, research and researchers who have succeeded have been validated through settler colonial structures of schooling and consequentially are answerable, minimally, to working to dismantle those structures (Hart, 2013, as quoted in Tierney, 2013; Jordan-Young, 2010). Educational researchers must, as one example, answer to ways in which the field has allowed learning to be lost in the pursuit of test-score-driven achievement. While test scores can indicate multiple realities, including cultural match or lack thereof, single metrics cannot robustly communicate learning, or even more precisely, areas of potential learning. With extant focus on test-score achievement, the field of educational research has drifted from the ways that any form of data is voided of meaning outside of its context.

Answerability means that we have responsibilities as speakers, listeners, and those responsibilities include stewardship of ideas and learning, ownership. As educational researchers, I believe we must stay attentive to three primary sets of coordinates, themselves each impermanently fixed but durable enough to afford a better reckoning with social, political, and material locations of educational research.

Answerable to Learning

First and foremost, educational research is answerable to learning. Learning should not, however, be mistaken to be synonymous with schooling. Schooling is an institution in society, as explored in extant sociological and educational studies literature, that is more successful at societal stratification than any other sector or educational project in the United States (Anyon, 1980; Bowles and Gintis, 2011). Schooling has historically and contemporarily served the purposes of reifying whiteness (Grande, 2004), as a location of settler colonialism. Under these auspices, learning has become disturbingly conflated with achievement within schools. In recent trends of neoliberal, corporate-backed education reforms, scores on large-scale standardized assessments coupled with generalized core curricula conjoin to reseat Eurocentric histories and perspectives (Kumashiro, 2010). Very little of this has anything to do with learning. While there are instances of teachers and young people in myriad locations who craft out spaces to reclaim, interrogate, and regenerate learning amidst reductionist–technicist definitions of learning (e.g., Nieto, 2014), generally, education and, complementarily, educational research have become servile to achievement in schooling, which need not include any learning. If learning, then, is not achievement on whitestream assessments in Euro-centered curricula taught by Euro-descendant teachers, what is it? This is the first place where educational researchers must engage in productive undoing and destabilization to become better stewards. Educational researchers will have to look through unfamiliar eyes at recent far-reaching and well-funded federal policies like No Child Left Behind and Race to the Top to disambiguate learning from test-score achievement. While some educational research may have been considerate of achievement in schools, it is dubious if those efforts interrupted settler logics of property, material acquisition, and ownership. Out of laudable intentions to not want students to fall prey to the increased vulnerability that often accompanies lower educational attainment, educational researchers have inconsistently interrogated the ways that a system built on stratification will refuse widespread achievement. Put another way, if the achievement gap in schooling could be closed, how would this be met within a society that is, by long-standing design and increasingly widened, fundamentally stratified. Because wholesale assimilation is counter to the system itself, learning has become a shameful location of collateral damage in the interest of test-score production.

Being answerable to learning deserves a more sophisticated centering of what learning is, in its various manifestations. The study, theorizing, and praxis of learning is where integrity should hold for educational researchers. How educational research serves learning provides a place to more fully embody decolonial stances, as it has the potential to materially alter how educational research is conducted and for what purposes. I propose a repositioning towards learning, an alteration of researching bodies in places. For this, I must draw on work largely outside educational research. This is not to say that there aren't many examples of vibrant learning that come from schooling spaces. Projects of cultural revitalization that many Indigenous communities have crafted (e.g., Battiste, 2013; McCarty and Lee, 2014) provide excellent role models not to be mimicked but to learn from, for lessons about cultural survivance, learning as a community priority, and learning for growth. Before compromised efforts to racially integrate schooling spaces (Bell, 1979), many all-Black communities exhibited some of the most vibrant community-based and self-sufficient learning spaces, despite fiscally disadvantaged conditions (Espinoza and Vossoughi, 2014). Beyond K-12 settings, community-based learning collectives have exhibited traits of self-determination, not just for individuals but also for collectives. These examples and studies all point to the ways that all populations, even those historically marginalized know learning, even though they may not consistently know success in formal schooling. But the vast majority of educational research, particularly that which has been traditionally best and most profitably sanctioned with awards, high-status journal publications, and grant endowments, has focused on achievement within Eurocentric contexts, without questioning that Eurocentric focus.

Learning is fundamentally about transformation. It is coming into being and constantly altering that being; it is a subjective and often messy act. It is, in essence, letting go of a rung we have a firm grip on in order to fumble with the specter of a different rung. Coming into being is in essence about being-in-relation. In her study of the places of learning found in media, architecture, and pedagogy, Elizabeth Ellsworth (2004) draws attention to the fundamentally transitional space that is learning. Rather than how the tradition of schooling has materially designed conditions for the transmittal and disciplined mimicry of expert knowledge, and educational research has in turn and in cahoots truncated learning to be measureable achievement meant to be predicted, Ellsworth encourages the reader to think about the conditions that make learning possible but still unpredictable. She follows the traditions of thinkers like Grosz (1995), Massumi (2002), and Winnicott (2005), who attend to the social self as one in constant motion, constantly reconfiguring itself, learning in relation to time, space, and materiality. She writes:

> Learning never takes place in the absence of bodies, emotions, place, time, sound, image, self-experience, history. It always detours through memory, forgetting, desire, fear, pleasure, surprise, rewriting. And because learning takes place in relation, its detours take us up to and sometimes across the boundaries of habit, recognition, and the socially constructed identities within ourselves.
>
> (p. 55)

Through several examples, Ellsworth draws our attention to, in part, the interior changes that museum spaces were designed for pedagogically (Eakle, 2009). For example, in discussing how the Civil Rights Museum in Birmingham, Alabama, sets up exterior conditions for interior alterity, Ellsworth (2004) writes, such places of learning implicate bodies in pedagogy in ways that the field of education has seldom explored. As they do this, they encourage and challenge us to move away from understanding the learning self merely through notions of cognition, psychology, or phenomenology, or as being subjected to ideology.

(p. 6)

Core to this framing is learning as a constant becoming and unbecoming, a constant inquiry and coordinate-taking, which sounds a lot like what research is supposed to be. Such a stance opens up spaces to depart from paradigms that theorize freedom, here to learn, as defined relative to restrictions, as in freedom from, but rather freedom as expansive, as in freedom to (Grosz, 1994). Learning and knowledge, then, are better approached, particularly in the name of decolonization, as fundamentally nomadic (Deleuze, 1978; Roy, 2005), refusing our well-worn brackets and borders of age/grade assumptions, subject area dominance, and still dominant modernist ideas about identity (Gordon, 1997; Sandoval, 2000).

Consider another example of learning, also imbued with research, this one from choreography (W. Rhodes, personal communication, 2009). In 2009, an actor named Gregg Mozgala started to work with choreographer Tamar Rogoff (Genzlinger, 2009). Mozgala has cerebral palsy, and Rogoff has no formal understanding of the biology, neuroscience, or physical therapy knowledges of cerebral palsy. But their way of working together and taking cues from his body, rather than working around it, altered deeply his way of being with his body. And what they did was use the principles of research – looking, inquiring, keeping track, and doing it all over again constantly. Like the pauses noted at the start of this volume, meaning making and performance was interrupted, slowed down, with observation and biofeedback to return again. This created the space for learning and knowledge production. More specifically, Rogoff introduced Mozgala to a tension-releasing shaking technique. They began doing intensive one-on-one sessions of body work, Rogoff using her knowledge of the body and dance-training techniques to help Mozgala "find" individual bones, muscles and tendons that he had thought had become simply relegated to collateral damage of the cerebral palsy. Much of this, in the medical field, would be understood to be evidence of neuroplasticity, and while it certainly is, it also speaks fundamentally to what research is. It is contextual, it is about constant coordination of self with other, self within self, and it is in constant motion.

Answerable to Knowledge

At the most basic definition, research is the pursuit of knowledge. While it is commonplace in Western higher education to define research as the production of knowledge, this definition has an implicit researcher-centric way of defining the existence of knowledge; that it does not manifest until someone has discovered it, which conjures a problematic echo of the colonial project of discovery. This is a subtle yet significant difference from the ways that I have earlier suggested an orientation to coming-into-beings. Knowledge does not exist decontextualized from those who are trying to know, but that is also different from considering how skills or practices had meaning to others before one happens upon them.

Take, for example, how a particular worldview is communicated in a recent *Newsweek* article on languages that plants use (Mejia, 2014) whose headline reads, "Speaking in (Green) Tongues: Scientist Discovers New Plant Language." The new is only relative to the researcher; it's not necessarily new to the plants, but by labeling it as new, there is an implicit anthropocentrism and researcher-centric yield to knowledge that is not necessarily for humans, or made into existence only by its measurement by humans.

One of the key challenges to educational research, to much of research that has emanated from settler colonial logics is to destabilize anthropocentricity. As Sylvia Wynter (2003) details in her piece that explores the origins of colonial projects of distinction, early projects of coloniality determined aspects of the planet (e.g., the heavens), to be of higher stature, and other parts, lands inhabited by Indigenous peoples, to be themselves corrupt. These designations of corrupt and lesser land were strategically shifted, eventually invisibilized, when colonial desire for the lands arose. While tropes of taming both wild land and Native peoples abound, the association of the land as inherently lesser was erased through colonial settlement. While there is much to consider from Wynter's work, and this is only a light skimming of its depth, here I focus on how nonhuman entities are known through human-centered, more specifically European-male-centered referents. And this pattern is ubiquitous, even within ecology-centered views.

In *The Botany of Desire*, botanist Michael Pollan (2001) explores the relationships among four types of plants, their relative appeal to human beings, and the adaptive and maladaptive connective tissue between plants and animals. For example, in framing his exploration of how apple plants maximized sweetness to be more protected, cultivated, and, in essence, sanctioned by humans, Pollan poses that plants have an "existential crisis," in that they are rooted in place, they cannot move of their own volition. Pollan uses this frame to illustrate how apple plants shift qualities of their fruit by virtue of which the qualities lead to their sustenance, even proliferation. Pollan's work is scintillating and exciting, because of its attention to assemblages, to co-evolution. However, Pollan implicitly perpetuates an anthropocentric view of nonhuman beings, which compromises the laudable goal in his cumulative work of persuading human beings to eat in more planet-responsible ways. In his appeal to help humans understand the deep, fluctuating, and quixotic relationships among plants and humans, Pollan runs the risk of obscuring plants' ways of being and in the interest of using anthropomorphic metaphors to engage the reader. What do we miss, though, both in terms of overestimating control and misunderstanding dynamics, through this default to anthropocentrism? Instead, researchers can both pursue and steward knowledge, but as fundamentally related to other knowledge and not only in terms of human goals. This challenge runs across the board to researchers, and the coordinates for educational researchers are specific to the field of learning in addition to the more widespread shifts in knowledge that are necessary.

If we are to be other than owners invested in settler colonialism, educational research needs a radical restructuring of its relationship to knowledge. Rather than property, we should see knowledge, and more specifically knowledge about learning, as what we are answerable to. We should see ourselves as stewards not of specific pieces of knowledge but rather of the productive and generative spaces that allow for finding knowledge. But we must also learn to regard all knowledge as incomplete, partial, contextually created, and perspectival. Perhaps the greatest contribution, that has also acted as collateral damage, that the field of qualitative research committed was to claim its stance of perspectival research. This is a vital contribution to knowledge itself, as all research, all forms of measuring, are perspectival and intra-active. Yet, when this is claimed as part of qualitative research, large-scale, inferential quantitative statistical designs, for example, are not held accountable for how they, likewise, are partial, perspectival, impacted, and impacting upon their contexts. Consider again Barad's example of technology used in medical fields and how an object largely seen to be inanimate is continually shaped by myriad material forces. This example, from the "hard" sciences, when understood through the rigorous analytics of quantum physics, reveals the deeply contextualized and mutable use of an instrument so that we can see the instrument itself is contextually constituted and mutable. Barad's work and examples, palatable to understanding Western technologies, similarly are limited in understanding technologies that are more explicitly in concert with ethnoecologies (Kawagley, 2006 [1995]) of well-being and balance.

All knowledge, all ways of knowing, are subject to the same temporalities and sets of impermanence. But such an understanding is all but contrary to how educational research is typically framed in the academy. Novice researchers learn to discuss their study's limitations in terms of its nongeneralizability, to apologize for its specifics. This does a disservice both to the omnipresent limited nature of any research set but also to the affordances that a particular study may lend. It works from the implicit premise that research should be universal, generalizable, and immutable, key constructs of coloniality. Instead, knowledge should be seen as an entity, specific, mutable, and impermanent itself. Such a regard does not mean to resign ourselves to a less than desirable form of knowledge but a more realistic one that can ask better questions. Instead of asking how to pursue mythical objective truth (which is a facade for coloniality), we can ask what knowledge might be useful at this moment, in this place, and how does our pursuit of it stay attentive to its material effects? This will involve, necessarily, giving up some of the mantle of expert and/but offers a stewardship of knowledge that follows self, or put more in more quotidian language, ego.

Being answerable to knowledge as related to other knowledges will require, though, a shift from the ways that the academy supports specialized knowledge in ways that make it difficult for specialists to be in conversation with each other (Macedo, 2000). Just as with the radical reconfiguration to learning as transformation, seeing knowledge as relational, being answerable to knowledge as fundamentally partial and impermanent, also requires a core shift in the ways that researchers pursue and communicate knowledge. As an example, each writer, each researcher who is writing, must consider the tone of their writing. Doctoral students learn implicitly, and sometimes explicitly, how authority, expertise, and ownership of knowledge are communicated linguistically in academic writing. They learn how to write their thoughts without ever referencing themselves, so that universality is prioritized over particularity. To write and value particularity and relationality, then, means that in just that one stream of academic apprenticeship and work, wider expressions of expertise will have to be recognized, to then be validated and able to transform institutionalized ways of knowing.

Answerable to Context

In addition to being answerable to learning and knowledge, educational research is answerable to context. Because learning is fundamentally about transformation and coming-into-being happens in context, this transformation is always situated in context. What then, are the ways that context must always be considered as part of educational research?

As detailed in Chapter 3 in the essay addressing what the Zimmerman verdict has to do with education, educational research is answerable to the ways that schooling has acted as a conduit for intertwined systems of oppression, including racist capitalism, heteropatriarchy, and ableism. There are many ways that addressing this context occurs in educational research, but with often muted or muddled theories of change.

For example, extant studies explore interventions for closing the achievement gap, yet not many of those studies contend with the tight alignment between academic achievement gap trends and related public policies on racial segregation, housing, and social services. Trends and patterns in educational practices and outcomes are never outside of other trends in society. As is often noted, the increasing policies of zero tolerance in school (for drugs, for weapons, for aberrations from dress codes, etc.) and resultant suspensions and expulsions are tightly connected to incarceration rates. Yet, in fewer instances is schooling theorized and studied as a holding location that is coordinated with other sites of containment. More recent scholarship has begun to make those connections (Krueger-Henney, 2014; Stovall, 2016; Gilmore, 2006).

However, being answerable to context does not only mean attending to the historical and ongoing destruction of colonialism. Additionally, it means attending to the ways that humans and nonhumans in various contexts engage in learning as potential, as sustenance, as fugitive (Espinoza and Vossoughi, 2014). My articulations of learning as transformation are themselves linked to and refusing definitions of learning as static and therefore imminently subject to metrics. As such, my articulation is also referential; it should be not be seen as universal or permanent. It is permeable and its resultant shifts in contexts will shed light on how and what kinds of departures are appropriate.

Being answerable to context dynamically helps to illuminate what kinds of knowledges are important. Projects of systemic social change cannot pursue knowledge without regard to the context they are trying to change. For example, the Black student union movement in the 1960s helped to erode structural racism on the campuses of higher education in the United States (Biondi, 2012), not permanently or pervasively, but the organizing work of those young people laid pathways, similar to older generations of activists. In doing so, they had to develop strategies for the pursuit of knowledge that facilitated their goals, which had everything to do with white structural power, including knowing how many Black students were enrolled on campus. This may seem like a simple area to pursue, but in fact, students gaining access to enrollment information, particularly Black students, is far from a simple feat. It required multiple levels of strategies, yet it was important because of the context in which these students' goals were developed. The students were answerable to context in how they pursued knowledge.

Similarly, the current undocumented youth movement holds compelling examples of how an attention and answerability to context shapes pursuit of knowledge. Undocumented youth, who number roughly 11 million in the United States, are defined not through any single ethnicity or race but through their liminality, at the margins in every setting that requires legal documentation in the United States. This sizeable yet marginalized entity is one of the most publicly engaged groups of youth in the nation, participating in and enacting forms of pedagogy in private and public settings. The prominent role of immigrant youth in the massive rallies for immigration rights in 2006 and the recent push for the DREAM Act, signal their growing social impact. Undocumented youth have organized around their common social location relative to policies that bar them from social opportunities, most notably but not limited to, access to in-state tuition rates in higher education. To impact policies, they have formed multiracial, multiethnic activist groups and have used various public actions, such as rallies, to both educate and shift the opinions of various stakeholders. Within their meeting spaces and in public demonstrations, undocumented youth engage in pedagogies and research those pedagogies out of answerability to changing social contexts.

I offer these extra-educational examples not to barter in tacit anti-intellectualism or to imply that deep, rigorous, discipline-specific study is unimportant, but to promote a radical reconfiguration of being and being-in-relation-to knowledge and learning, to foreground how fundamental a shift and re-setting should be undertaken to strip off the layers of the colonial view of education. However, radical reconfigurations require vigilance, particularly in an era where proxies can be used-lots of complex dynamics, masking durable harmful patterns. In the next chapter, I take up the example of racialization and how it has been harmfully adopted in educational research, as well as researchers who address it in keeping with anticolonial purposes.

References

Ahmed, S. (2006). *Queer Phenomenology: Orientations, Objects, Others*. Durham, NC: Duke University Press.

Anyon, Jean (1980). Social Class and the Hidden Curriculum of Work. *The Journal of Education 162*(1): 67–92.

Bakhtin, Mikhael (1986). *Speech Genres and Other Late Essays* (Vern W. McGee, Trans.). Austin, TX: University of Texas Press.

Baldwin, J. (1963). My Dungeon Shook: Letter to My Nephew on the One Hundredth Anniversary of the Emancipation. In: *The Fire Next Time*. New York: Dial Press, p. 21.

Barad, Karen (2007). *Meeting the Universe Halfway: Quantum Physics and the Entanglement of Matter and Meaning*. Durham, NC: Duke University Press.

Battiste, M. (2013). *Decolonizing Education: Nourishing the Learning Spirit*. Saskatoon, Canada: Purich Publishing.

Bell Jr., D.A. (1979). *Brown v. Board of Education* and the Interest–Convergence Dilemma. *Harvard Law Review 93*: 518.

Biondi, M. (2012). *The Black Revolution on Campus*. Berkeley: University of California Press.

Bowles, S., and H. Gintis (2011). *Schooling in Capitalist America: Educational Reform and the Contradictions of Economic Life*. Reprint Edition. Chicago: Haymarket Books.

Deleuze, Gilles (1978). Nomad Thought. *Semiotexte 3*(1): 12.

Eakle, A.J. (2009). Museum Literacies and Adolescents Using Multiple Forms of Texts "On Their Own." *Journal of Adolescent & Adult Literacy 53*(3): 204–214.

Ellsworth, E. (2004). *Places of Learning: Media, Architecture, Pedagogy*. New York: Routledge.

Espinoza, Manuel Luis, and Shirin Vossoughi (2014). Perceiving Learning Anew: Social Interaction, Dignity, and Educational Rights. *Harvard Educational Review 84*(3): 285–313.

Genzlinger, N. (2009, November 25). Learning His Body, Learning to Dance. Accessed from: http://www.nytimes.com/2009/11/25/arts/dance/25palsy.html.

Gilmore, R.W. (2006). *Golden Gulag: Prisons, Surplus, Crisis, and Opposition in Globalizing California* (Vol. 21). Berkeley, CA: University of California Press.

Gordon, Avery (1997). *Ghostly Matters: Haunting and the Sociological Imagination*. Minneapolis, MN: University of Minnesota Press.

Grande, S. (2004). *Red Pedagogy: Native American Social and Political Thought*. New York: Rowman & Littlefield.

Grosz, E. (1994). *Volatile Bodies: Toward a Corporeal Feminism*. First Edition. Bloomington, IN: Indiana University Press.

Grosz, E.A. (1995). *Space, Time, and Perversion: Essays on the Politics of Bodies*. London: Routledge.

Jordan-Young, R.M. (2010). *Brain Storm: The Flaws in the Science of Sex Differences*. Cambridge, MA: Harvard University Press..

Kawagley, Angayuqaq Oscar (2006) [1995]. *A Yupiaq Worldview: A Pathway to Ecology and Spirit*. Second Edition. Long Grove, IL: Waveland Pr. Inc.

Krueger-Henney, P. (2014). Co-Researching School Spaces of Dispossession: A Story of Survival. *Association of Mexican American Educators Journal 7*(3): 42–53.

Kumashiro, K. (2010). *Teaching toward Democracy: Educators as Agents of Change*. Boulder, CO: Paradigm Publishers.

Macedo, Donaldo (2000). The Colonialism of the English Only Movement. *Educational Researcher 29*(3): 15–24.

Massumi, Brian (2002). *Parables for the Virtual: Movement, Affect, Sensation*. Durham, NC: Duke University Press.

McCarty, T., and T. Lee (2014). Critical Culturally Sustaining/Revitalizing Pedagogy and Indigenous Education Sovereignty. *Harvard Educational Review 84*(1): 101–124.

Mejia, D. 2014. Speaking in (Green) Tongues: Scientist Discovers New Plant Language. *Newsweek*. Accessed November 4, 2014 from: www.newsweek.com/speaking-green-tongues-scientist-discovers-new-plant-language-264734.

Nieto, Sonia (2014). *Why We Teach Now*. New York: Teachers College Press.

Pollan, Michael (2001). *The Botany of Desire: A Plant's-Eye View of the World*. New York: Random House.

Roy, K. (2005). Power and Resistance: Insurgent Spaces, Deleuze, and Curriculum. *Journal of Curriculum Theorizing 21*(1): 27.

Sandoval, Chela (2000). *Methodology of the Oppressed*. Minneapolis, MN: University of Minnesota Press.

Smith, Linda Tuhiwai (2012). *Decolonizing Methodologies: Research and Indigenous Peoples*. Second Edition. London and New York: Zed Books.

Stovall, D.O. (2016). *Born out of Struggle: Critical Race Theory, School Creation, and the Politics of Struggle*. Albany, New York: SUNY Press.

Tierney, J. (2013, September 16). The Rational Choices of Crack Addicts. Accessed from: http://www.nytimes.com/2013/09/17/science/the-rational-choices-of-crack-addicts.html.

Winnicott, D.W. (2005). *Playing and Reality*. Second Edition. London and New York: Routledge.

Wynter, S. (2003). Unsettling the Coloniality of Being/Power/Truth/Freedom: Towards the Human, after Man, Its Overrepresentation – an Argument. *Centennial Review 3*(3): 257–337.

5

BEYOND SOCIAL JUSTICE

In order for a phoenix to rise, from its own ashes, A phoenix must first burn down

(Octavia Butler)

this past was waiting for me
when i came
(Lucille Clifton)

Many years ago, an Advanced Qualitative Research class that I was teaching gathered to discuss Linda Tuhiwai Smith's book, *Decolonizing Methodologies* (2012). Tuhiwai Smith provides a bold, systemic analysis of the ways that research has been directed by and enacted colonization for millennia. In roughly two halves of the book, Tuhiwai Smith first shows how the consecutive and cumulative ways that research has dehumanized Indigenous peoples has led to a deep and well-seated distrust of research, and in the second half, she presents research conducted by Indigenous peoples who are guided by logics and ethics far afield from colonial scripts of ownership and property. I had split the reading of the book over two class sessions, to both follow the structure of the book and to allow time for readers new to the content to absorb the comprehensive and integrated history and ongoing project of colonialism in research.

As we convened to discuss the second half of the book, I asked the class for reactions to the book as a whole. A thick moment of silence ensued as we sat in our seminar circle, myself, and the six students, five European Americans, all of whom were monolingual, and one Latina, who grew up in a working class and bilingual community. Breaking the silence, one white woman in her late twenties offered this: "I just don't know what I'm supposed to do with all of this. She (Tuhiwai Smith) explains all of this but then she doesn't really give a way out." Several of the other students nodded.

Although it's been years since this exchange, it has lingered with me. I've thought a great deal about how it reflects and creates materiality – the material social positions, trajectories, and the material effects – in this response. Even a cursory read of Smith's final chapters in *Decolonizing Methodologies* contradicts this response, as the book includes examples and explanations of dozens of research projects designed and conducted by Indigenous peoples, listing both approaches and knowledge systems in these projects. The woman was and surely is not a person who was incapable of deep and rigorous reading. So her comment begs, in turn, a more robust reading of the meaning she was making and how it matters. I suggest that the meaning put forward by this student is multiple: that understanding oneself as part of colonial history and present is hard, that a reclamation and refusal of research is unsettling (for researchers, particularly those who might be refused), and that learning about research is cultural practice. Learning about research as a cultural practice, given the unseemly cultural and structural trajectories research has created, is itself counter to the colonialist concepts of knowledge as objectively rendered, neutral, and person-less. All of this is in, between, around, and after her desire to know what to do. It's possible that this felt impending in the final pages of a book addressing anticolonial educational research and perhaps was amplified when Smith's instances of decolonial research displayed examples done by and for Indigenous populations. While there are specifics involved in this woman's social location to the project of decolonizing methodologies, the impulse for action and for ideas to import action is not unique to her.

We particularly want to know what to do when we have come to know our own advantages, complicitness, and benefit from a system of coloniality that is structured on some having more than others. This is understandable in a time when systemic oppression is misunderstood, dysfunctionally, to reside in individuals, and therefore within cultures. This belief is conjoined with the terror of being labeled a racist. As Eduardo Bonilla-Silva theorized from his study of white college students, this is a time of racism without racists (2009). This context manifests in several truncated questions and interactions, for example, trying to name someone or some interaction as racist instead of understanding how racialization shapes all interactions. Such overly simplistic separations between racists and nonracists often emanates from desires for innocence, evidenced in reactions to critiques of systemic oppression that maintain the innocence of some members of a privileged group, such as the Twitter hashtags #notallmen and #alllivesmatter. Such reactions work to evade the structural nature of oppression in favor of protecting some as external, which implies better, to these conditions. The context of individualism and racism without racists, or an overt policing of political correctness, in essence inspires individuals to act in ways that are imagined to distance them from oppression. The material effect of this is that the structural nature of agents of oppression, such as pervasive patriarchy that objectifies women, receives less attention than innocentizing specific individuals.

Within this context that draws from individualized notions of oppression, it is little surprise that the desire for personal action comes quickly on the heels of systemic analysis. So quickly, in fact, that it ironically often muffles that analysis by conflating interpersonal interactions, for example, with the scope of structural oppression. The saying, "the personal is political," is an apt instantiation of this, drawing attention to individuals and their experiences, often at the expense of systemic analysis. Ashon Crawley noted (2014),

> "The personal" is often about the articulation of a set of infractions that make someone a victim, such that their sense of identity is grounded in such victimhood, and such victimhood becomes the shield against which no interrogation can occur. "The personal" is the elaboration of the bourgeois subject. And, then also on the other side of the "is," is a need for interrogating "the political." This concept is not neutral and has its own sets of problematics: political but towards what end? Are we attempting to become the political subject of the state?

The instantiation of the bourgeois state subject is not a given in the word "personal," but it takes on this almost exclusive resonance in societies grown from individualistic understandings of beings. Such individualism is also noted for its anthropocentrism, which insists upon the primacy of human beings as individuals under the state, with greater and lesser human rights. This is the core philosophic stance of democracy, human rights campaigns, and even different societal analysis models, including Marxism.

But, you might ask, why then put forward one student's response, if part of the point is to reject a dysfunctional collapse of the systemic into the individual? Why one student's utterance from the dozen unique occasions I've taught this advanced methods course? If we default to the well-worn, and yes, colonial constructs of research, we might ask if it's offered because of its representativeness. Has her response been (and implicatively will it be) uttered by others, regardless of place or context? Therein lies the assertion of colonial erasures of place and the connectedness of all knowledge to place. The very concept of representativeness relies on a tacit Euclidean linearity and predictability of human practices given a sample of practices (Davis and Sumara, 2009). This is in opposition to the stance that knowledge is linked to place (Tuck and McKenzie, 2014). As much as representativeness and predictability are dominant in research traditions, linear representativeness need not be why a practice, action, or utterance is considered.

More than representative I regard this student's comment as important because it's referential. It samples. It referenced many patterns and took on a particular shape in this context. Students of hip hop implicitly understand that a sample neither rests in the original song nor the resultant remix; it operates in a newly created space that is tied to both. The student's comment mattered in our gathering in that it had material effect on what was discussable and it brought with it historical trajectories of responsibility with unknown possibilities for how we could engage with the comment. Similar comments matter in the extant anti-racism workshops that end up being dominated by white voices, in the conversations about gender that are governed by cisgender people, and in the ways that feminism has historically silenced intersectional contributions because they agitate the race privilege of white women. When the student asked what "we" are supposed to do and thereby asserted that options weren't provided in the book, she recentered herself and those outside of Indigenous communities, as the primary users and creators of research, and in this instance, purportedly, the primary people not addressed by Smith's work. I wonder if she did this precisely because of the centering of research done by and for Indigenous peoples that Smith highlights in the second half of the book? We are not likely to know, but it is likely that her frustration was linked to not having her specific positionality reflected in the second half of the book.

The comment is also referential to pragmatism. We want a "do this, not this," and we come by this wanting honestly, in the sense that it is a well-socialized way of being in the world. Pragmatism, the principle that an idea or concept is inherently better with an understanding of what it will do or does, is often attributed to being a pre-eminently American way of being and doing. Pragmatism is often mis-attributed to European settlers on Turtle Island (Pratt, 1991), but in fact this epistemology and ontology, having a sense of function driving form, long precedes European invasion of Turtle Island. The erasure of Native pragmatism is but one in a long and ongoing set of erasures that are fundamental to the historical and ongoing structure of settler colonialism. Settler colonialism is most finitely described as the ongoing need to erase Indigenous peoples, and wrest humanity from Black peoples, in order to jam the frequency of the settler colonist's settling. Sociohistorically and as an ongoing cultural set of practices, then, the desire for action, for an idea to have worth in what it means and what it does, cannot be dismissed lightly, and it is not my intention in this chapter to wave a hand at the desire for action as in and of itself petty. I ask, instead, in keeping with research being in relation, what is the political economy of desired and enacted action relative to its sociopolitical contexts?

While there are some instructions and directives that are often taken to be preferable for learning, the strongly held methods fetish in research generally and also within educational research should minimally inspire caution in a rush to action. Particularly within education and educational research, with our methods fetish (Bartolomé, 1994) and tendency to default to technicism (Luke, 1991), the impulse to action should be considered as a site with deep potential for transformation. That impulse to act may be part of what can be used, perhaps counterintuitively, to unsettle the very settler colonial logics that should be dismantled. In other words, it may be in the wanting to do but not leaping into doing that we can excavate the underlying principles and taken-for-granteds that so often end up reconstituting settler colonialism as a structure.

In that spirit, I want to suggest that perhaps the best move that educational researchers can do, in the interest of decolonialization, that is to say eradicating, dismantling, and obliterating colonialism, is to pause in order to reach beyond, well beyond, the most familiar of tropes in education and educational research. I suggest that we entertain, quite pragmatically, what we need to stop and that without that stoppage it is actually impossible to imagine how to do differently. I heed the analysis of other thinkers including bell hooks and Arundhati Roy who maintain that it is premature, impulsive, and counterproductive to demand the details, blueprint, and figured world alter-realities of decolonization when our current context is so deeply embedded and enlived by colonial logics. I chose to open this closing chapter with this vignette and analysis precisely because referents to the individual and personhood are replete in the exchange, and require a thoughtful consideration to dismantle these defaults in the interest of countering coloniality.

Perhaps one of the most explicit decolonial moves we can make, at this moment, is to sit still long enough to see clearly what we need to reach beyond. This stillness should not be confused with doing nothing. Without pause, it's difficult to ascertain what structures, what inequitable structures, are enlivened by narratives, even and perhaps especially the progressive narratives. Our pauses, actions, and revisiting should be answerable to a constant desire for material transformation, repatriation, and rectification. In so doing, though, we have to consider what tools of progress, however inadvertently, have become conduits and proxies (Perry, 2011) for settler logics and have themselves become part of the structure of settler colonialism. Just as learning has become conflated with test-score measures of achievement, the moral goal of formal education also must be examined. To close this book, I offer another pause, but this time with the provocation that quieting a prevalent discourse will create space and allow for the imagination and emergence of conceptual and praxis shapes. I believe we have to pause, to suspend (Tuck, 2009) the use of social justice in educational research because it has become a vehicle for settler logics and heteropatriarchal racist capitalism.

A Moratorium on Social Justice

Now how can I pick on social justice? It is the mantle and platform of many progressive educators and social scientists, often bearing the ill-placed critique of being ideological, which situates it poorly within a field that values objectivity as a knowledge-for project (Wynter, 2003). Most often, mission statements for schools that address social justice include language of democracy, inclusion, equity, and diversity. Who in their right minds could ever possibly have a problem with social justice when it seems to be explicitly counter to imbalances of power? Does this mean I am outing myself as a Fox News aficionado, as a one percenter, or as a cynic who believes oppression and stratification to be unavoidable, endemic to society? Far from it.

I suggest that we must pause and reconsider social justice precisely because it has a hold on educational research, appearing so ubiquitously as to carry sizable assumptions of goals and approaches. When a platform is so ubiquitous, the chances are strong that it may actually be holding untenable positions within its wholesale sweep. When so much of societal structures are facilitated by widely held narratives, such as meritocracy, the narrative itself should be routinely and lovingly scrutinized for what it might be facilitating, intended or not. The love I speak of here is not romantic love but the generative love that is crucial for radical transformation. Social justice, as a ubiquitous frame of education and educational research, is often connected to human rights but far less frequently addresses relationships across peoples, land, and cultures.

One of the most compelling aspects of settler colonialism as a theoretical framework is that it articulates the specific and unique positions of peoples and land that are differentially needed to maintain the structure. In consideration of settler colonialism's specific needs for differential locations of vulnerability, erasure, and dehumanization, concepts like "inclusion" and "equity" seem dismally insufficient. Inclusion in what and on what terms? Equitable in terms of what? Access to land? Land as property, as resource, as teacher, as parent, as child? When viewed in relation to the complicated history of land, settling, and chattel labor, platforms of justice that seek equal treatment for human beings are, at best, off-kilter. Without direct engagement of the connections across entities set asunder and dispossessed by settler colonialism, the anthropocentric liberal humanism found in much of social justice reseats certain settler logics, with the far reach of justice being a subject of the state, at best a better treated subject of the state. As Lisa Marie Cacho (2012) theorizes, statelessness is purposefully facilitated and created within frames of liberal humanism, guaranteeing that some are entitled to racialized statehood because others are not. In such ubiquity and with such wide assumptions that obscure the specifics of social locations and areas of contradiction, social justice has worked to reseat settler logics, situating people as subjects of the state, itself above land. In short, it has become a brand that acts as proxy for institutionalized progressivism. Not disconnected from the ways that affirmative action agendas in higher education are promoted out of an interest of diversity for learning rather than countering systemic and intertwined forms of advantage for white men, social justice can be equated with diversity but not decentering cultures of privilege. With such projects of inclusion but not transformation, imaginative space is literally foreclosed to radically transform the terms of co-existence. In suspending that foreclosure, then, a pause reaches beyond doing nothing to being able to see the terms and enactments of the foreclosure. By pausing or distancing from social justice, though, I do not suggest an embargo on the term, social justice, or any term, wholesale.

As a lifelong reader and writer who is comfortable with the idea that all language is metaphorical as well as the postmodern affordance that signifier and signified are not turgidly coupled, I cannot and do not dismiss any terms as wholesale corrupt or craven. Rather, I suggest taking a step back from social justice, a stronghold in educational research projects, schools of education and their mission statements, in order to see how it has mattered in distinctly colonial ways. In particular, I suggest a suspension of the uses of social justice because in often truncated leverages, the term has come to be a proxy for heteropatriarchal racist logics of individuality, a project that cannot dismantle coloniality because it was created to foment it. Rather than being opposed to social justice, which could be understood to be an "anti-" stance, I suggest a decolonial approach, which must fundamentally involve dismantling. Dismantling is different from simply opposing, an act that relies on a linear view of sociogeny. Rather, social relations are far from linear; they are concurrent, contradictory, and multimodal. To oppose imagines that there is a single face or point that can be made to rest still and then be unitarily countered. The leap of faith that I take is that in dismantling and transgressing the predominant frame of social justice, other possibilities, currently cauterized by the discourses of social justice, will emerge.

Social justice most broadly and perhaps most widely defined, is understood to be the quest for the realignment and rectification of societal inequities. There are extant images, mission statements, and quotes that offer definitions of social justice, with a simple web search revealing over 42 million results for the phrase, "social justice mission." How social justice actually takes shape, that is the theories of perhaps transformation, but certainly the theories of change (Tuck, 2009), found within those mission statements, within educational research projects, and the language and practices take on shape and in turn shape those texts. For example, most often, educational research that links to social justice focuses on populations that have been historically dispossessed (Fine and Ruglis, 2009). However, the suite of terms that are used to name this population speaks both of the often tacit theories of societal structure and the theories of change, of altering those material realities.

Consider this list of labels that are used in educational research:

- Underrepresented
- At-risk
- Minority
- English Language Learner
- Disadvantaged

While there are many more terms that are used to name and not name populations and systems that stratify their proximity to well-being (Gilmore, 2007), I focus on these partly because they are widespread in educational research and because they also all share a tacit theorization of social justice as inclusion, particularly in terms of quantity and presence. These terms and the mission statements, research projects, and analysis that are connected to them tend towards a goal of an egalitarian society, one in which individuals have equal, or equitable presence and representation in institutions in society. For example, the term underrepresented (a particularly popular term that acts as a proxy for racially minoritized peoples) speaks of a theory that social justice can be achieved through more equitable, or more equal, or certainly at least different amounts of people from various backgrounds in an institutional entity.

It is inarguable that a concentration of wealth and property ownership in a small segment of the population, historically and contemporarily, segments and stratifies society, and this concentration of well-being has sociohistorical roots and investment in whiteness as property (Harris, 1993) and more fundamentally coloniality (Wynter, 2003). However, it is nonetheless a fundamental and harmful truncation of analysis to assume that shifting, in this case, the racial composition of those included in certain sectors of society will result in material transformation of well-being. Put more simply, changing the composition of a group doesn't change the terms of the group automatically. The goal of including more historically marginalized people has within it a theory of change that invokes the racism-without-racists idea that colonialism, in this case specifically, racism, resides in some individuals but not in others, as opposed to being scripted and transcripted into a system built on stratification that impacts everyone, but to necessarily differing effects. It also, by default, reseats institutions as innocent or removed from the societal patterns of oppression and domination. Diversity is desired, but to improve the institution through representation, through heuristics, not to fundamentally alter or dismantle the settler logics of white supremacy and heteropatriarchy.

Moreover, diversity and inclusion are used as proxies to avoid naming whiteness and white supremacy as systemic structures that are animated through the law's imaginative limiting of individual rights. It is only within this logic that it is remotely logical to use the term "minority" for a population that accounts for roughly 75 percent of the planet's human beings. The term, minority, as with underrepresented, defaults to a frame of whiteness and obscures processes that racially minoritize and majoritize. These processes work at population levels but within liberal humanist discourses of social justice, with the collateral impact of the frames defaulting to individualized rights from the state.

As extant intersectional research and theorization details (Crenshaw, 1991; Cho, 2008; Spade, 2013), individual rights and individual nodes of personhood have been one of the most successful ways that the law has codified settler logics of whiteness. In his piece addressing intersectional resistance, activist and legal scholar Dean Spade articulates how the movement for marriage equality acts as a conduit for flawed projects of inclusion to a system designed to exclude:

> Terms like "marriage equality," the most common name used by advocates for the campaign to legalize same-sex marriage, expose the limitations of the framework. Marriage is fundamentally about inequality – about privileging and incentivizing certain family structures and making those

who live outside them more vulnerable. Single-axis demands for equality in lesbian and gay rights politics, then, come to look more like demands for the racial and class privilege of a narrow sector of lesbians and gay men to be restored so that they might pass their wealth on as they choose when they die, shield it from taxation, call the police to protect it, and endorse or join invading armies to expand it.

(2013, p. 1042)

While Spade's example is focused on the ways that marriage equality defaults to liberal ideals of individually metered equality based on deservingness, and that as an access point to connected wealth accumulation, his intersectional analysis is applicable, sadly, to the ways that rights in education have similarly been theorized as individual, anthropocentric, and state-afforded.

Consider the contrast to affirmative action programs as they were designed to rectify, through remediation, centuries upon centuries of systemic anti-blackness. In the last several Supreme Court hearings about the use of affirmative action programs in university admissions, there are few referents to this genesis (Poon, 2013). Rather, affirmative action has become misidentified, and yet still countered, as a way for institutions to achieve (racial) diversity, for the interest of the institution as a space of learning. Racially diverse student populations are sought not because there are intertwined systemic barriers to societal well-being for racially minoritized peoples but because the institution's interests are better served through a presentation of diversity (Ahmed, 2012). This communicates an underlying mythology of institutions, that at least here in the United States, they are believed to be, inherently, places of opportunity. Schooling, for example, still figures prominently in the public imagination as a place where social mobility can be, if not achieved, made much more possible. It also defaults to individual metrics of equality, calculating and truncating material difference through individual units (e.g., how many people of color are included in x or y institution). The result is a tautological approach that seeks pathways through the very structure created to stratify and categorize (N. Drane, personal communication).

Diversity, often the named goal of social justice programs, has come to mean a synthetic creation of mixed populations, for the benefit of the institution. Critical theorist and activist Kýra (2015) explained the connection across diversity, inclusion, and whiteness this way:

> Diversity is the practice of mixing together different bodies within a common organization, and is a prime resource to be capitalized upon by businesses and organizations that are white owned and/or operated. Diversity still benefits those in power by taking advantage of the various experiences and vantage points of different racial/gender/sexual backgrounds. Rather than respecting difference and redistributing power based on it, diversity only "celebrates" difference in order to exploit multiculturalism for its economic value.

None of this is to say that diversity is not good, but rather that such a binaristic statement or goal is woefully inadequate for a project of decolonization. Decolonization requires radical dismantling and disruption. That must include attending to the material effects of practices. Projects of inclusion, which are manifest in educational research on underrepresented, at-risk, minority, or even marginalized populations, contain within them tacit projects of deculturalization because they do not explicitly address interrupting material accumulation through dispossession. Deculturalization is a way to reseat property rights and whiteness, which are extensions of settler logics. From a stance of decolonization, inclusion is itself a violent premise, one that capitulates to a society based on stratified ownership, erasure of indigeneity, and that uses proxies to invisibilize white settler claims (inclusion is named but who cedes the terms of inclusion is not). This is a reality intimately experienced by every Indigenous person who must lodge a claim of their Native ancestry with the settler federal government. As noted in Chapter 2, the federal government created legal calculations of blood quantum and one-drop rules for African ancestry, two seemingly contradictory racial logics, for the overriding project of settler colonialism. Inclusion, then, should be met minimally with justifiable suspicion.

Education is, however, steeped in this approach to social justice, such that social justice has become another part of the colonial structure that suffocates exploration and imagination beyond logics of individuals, land property, and decontextualized knowledge. How could educational research approach decolonization without wresting itself from the ways it has come to occupy, reorganize, and refresh settler logics, through even its most liberal platform, that of social justice?

Educational research sits within a society that has centuries-long histories of coloniality as well as contemporary re-organizations of oppression and violence that demand nimble attention. To dismantle this, educational research will have to reckon with how devolution, that is the systemic reorganization and retrenchment of imperialist violence (Gilmore, 2014), has occurred throughout society. Specifically, and related to the discussion of inclusion, diversity, and equity, decolonial education researchers must be attentive to what Jodi Melamed (2006) terms official anti-racisms. Melamed identifies these knowledge systems as deracializing inequality on the one hand, while constructing neoliberal subject positions amenable to racialized processes of disinvestment, dispossession, and discipline on the other. For example, studies of school integration and desegregation must attend not just to the racial composition and diversity of students within a building but also to the patterns of referrals for special education, extramural programming, and structural places that frequently arise within these "inclusive" settings. As another example, what are the psychic loads that students of color carry in predominantly white institutions, and how does that manifest into structural inequity? Put another way, are schools positioned to consider what ways they are part of the burden of oppression documented in the *Unnatural*

Causes (California Newsreel, 2008) documentary? Situating Melamed's work calls for an extension of concepts like stereotype threat (Steele, 1997) and double consciousness (DuBois, 1903) to structural coordinates of oppression. Building a decolonial praxis of educational research requires that it dismantle its vested interests in colonial logics, in the implicit theories of assimilation that manifest in deculturalization and projects of deracination that reseat white material advantage.

While we pause and learn to unlearn and relearn the ready scripts of justice so ubiquitous throughout educational research, I assert we must also try to remind formal institutions of what they have never fully known. Learning and knowledge predate coloniality. They are not creations of coloniality nor are they doomed to only serve coloniality. They have simply been hijacked for those purposes. Educational researchers who seek decolonial praxes would do well to remember, from their specific social locations and places, that knowledge is always place-specific. The first move of coloniality (Wynter, 2003) was to align some land spaces as savage, and others (the heavens) as holy. That began the first laceration of knowledge from place. Coloniality is paradoxically based in the tacit understanding that peoples, knowledges, and interconnectivity are always place-based. Coloniality created savagery in order to claim domain over it and the lands on which the then-named savages were living. Seeing this as a paradoxical and self-serving logic helps to unsettle the terms on which settler colonialism is based and maintained. The paradox can be ascertained through its project of knowledge for what purposes.

In keeping with its paradoxical yet purposeful laceration between land and beings, coloniality similarly approached learning not as transformational but through metrics. Most contemporarily, it has collapsed learning into test-score production with property ownership project pursuits for corporations that create tests, govern charter and private schools, and contract degreed consultants in those endeavors. But just as lands and beings cannot be savage by decree only, learning is not a transaction. It is transformational. It is a fundamentally fugitive act, one that tears down and leaves behind to reach beyond. It does all of this with the completely beautiful and terrifying lack of knowledge of what lays ahead.

> There is nothing new under the sun, but there are new suns
>
> (Octavia Butler)

> come celebrate with me that everyday something has tried to kill me and has failed
>
> (Lucille Clifton)

Consider again the student's response in the qualitative research class. In many ways, when I think back to the student's frustration at the lack of her place in Smith's discussion of decolonial methodologies, I consider it at that threshold of learning, of undoing, of transformation. Why wouldn't someone balk at the prospect of going into a conceptual and material space that perhaps hasn't thought about you, particularly when the solidity of objectivity, methods, and triangulation, provide much more concrete, and yes, pragmatic, immediate actions? So perhaps in this balk is the sound of forgotten remembrance of learning. Learning that isn't about techniques for interviewing, writing, analyzing, or implicating. Learning that isn't immediately demonstrable, and measureable, but that involves being between a known and unknown. In this way, I see this student's balk as that sweet spot so rife with possibility if it is attended to without script of how to end the unsureness but instead an imagination of what might be possible if everything we've normally done no longer makes any sense.

In essence, I am talking about learning as an act of futurity. Futurity is the imprint, the scent, the murmur of what is in the future. In that sense, it is actually unknowable in the immediate, as its discrete details are not available through current lenses. You can't map futurity; you can only map possible futurities. Learning, similarly, is an act of letting go of what one knows for what one does not yet know. To enter into learning as anything other than that, to seek bumper rails is to forestall transformation and futurity. Learning that holds tightly to what is presently known is to want the safety of assimilation, and sacrifices the much messier desire of transformation. However, as long as coloniality has been in existence, so has learning, and it's important to remember that not only has learning predated and will survive coloniality, but that it has existed despite, because of, and in defiance of coloniality. This is imminently obvious in both the settler state's attempts to outlaw literacy for enslaved African peoples and the communication codes developed and used despite these barriers. The barriers were no contest for the futurity that learning held.

In fact, remembrance of futurities' forbearance radically shifts what can be done in the current moment. While we cannot map the future, we can map possible futurities and do so with a reckoning of the past trajectories that give shape to the present realities. We can ask if the futures we imagine, if the learning we want to create space for, animates or interrupts settler logics. We can ask if the futurities are settler or decolonial. I opened this chapter with two quotes from radically different authors, in terms of genres, who have written similarly about coloniality and futurity. Poet Lucille Clifton's work addresses humanness and dignity amidst attempts to contain it. Her verse is sparse and creates spaciousness. Science fiction writer Octavia Butler's work is known for its harsh commentary on the futurities likely to unfold in ongoing projects of stratification as well as futurities of pluralism that extend beyond Black nationalism and white liberalism. This concluding chapter offers quotes from these authors as imprints of the possibilities that are made available when more specious projects are cast aside. Seeing projects like social justice as specious does not mean resigning ourselves to thin-skinnedness or pessimism that is afraid to dream beyond the current inequities. On the contrary, discarding settler logics requires both a bold grasp of their detailed precision and an avowed refusal to capitulate oneself, one's praxis, and one's imagination to coloniality. That is the challenge that educational research faces in decolonizing its work: to set aside the malignant and impossible settler projects of assimilation and integration and become answerable to learning.

References

Ahmed, S. (2012). *On Being Included: Racism and Diversity in Institutional Life*. Durham, NC and London: Duke University Press.

Bartolomé, Lilia I. (1994). Beyond the Methods Fetish: Toward a Humanizing Pedagogy. *Harvard Educational Review 64*(2): 173–194.

Bonilla-Silva, E. (2009). *Racism without Racists: Color-blind Racism and the Persistence of Racial Inequality in America*. Third Edition. Lanham, MD: Rowman & Littlefield.

Cacho, L.M. (2012). *Social Death: Racialized Rightlessness and the Criminalization of the Unprotected*. New York: NYU Press.

California Newsreel (2008). *Unnatural Causes: Is Inequality Making Us Sick?*

Cho, S. (2008). Post-racialism. *Iowa Law Review 94*: 1589.

Crawley, A. (2014). An Oversimplification of Words. Accessed from http://ashoncrawley.com/2014/01/28/an-oversimplification-of-words.

Crenshaw, K (1991). Mapping the Margins: Intersectionality, Identity Politics, and Violence against Women of Color. *Stanford Law Review 43*(6): 1241–1299.

Davis, B., and D. Sumara (2009). Complexity as a Theory of Education. *TCI (Transnational Curriculum Inquiry) 5*(2): 33–44.

DuBois, W.E.B. (1903). *The Souls of Black Folk: Essays and Sketches*. Chicago: A.C. McClurg & Co.

Fine, M., and J. Ruglis (2009). Circuits and Consequences of Dispossession: The Racialized Realignment of the Public Sphere for U.S. Youth. *Transforming Anthropology 17*(1): 20–33. http://doi.org/10.1111/j.1548-7466.2009.01037.x.

Gilmore, R.W. (2007). *Golden Gulag: Prisons, Surplus, Crisis, and Opposition in Globalizing California*. Berkeley, CA: University of California Press.

Gilmore, R.W. (2014, November 7). The Scope of Slavery. Keynote presentation at Harvard University.

Harris, C. (1993). Whiteness as Property. *Harvard Law Review 106*(8): 1709–1795.

Kýra (2015). How to Uphold White Supremacy by Focusing on Diversity and Inclusion. Accessed from: https://modelviewculture.com/pieces/how-to-uphold-white-supremacy-by-focusing-on-diversity-and-inclusion.

Luke, A. (1991). Literacies as Social Practices. *English Education 23*: 131–147.

Melamed, J. (2006). The Spirit of Neoliberalism: From Racial Liberalism to Neoliberal Multiculturalism. *Social Text 24*: 1–24.

Perry, I. (2011). *More Beautiful and More Terrible: The Embrace and Transcendence of Racial Inequality in the United States*. New York: NYU Press.

Poon, O.A. (2013). Think About It as Decolonizing Our Minds. In: S.D. Museus, D.C. Maramba, and R.T. Teranishi (Eds.) *The Misrepresented Minority: New Insights on Asian Americans and Pacific Islanders, and the Implications for Higher Education*. Sterling, VA: Stylus, p. 294.

Pratt, M.L. (1991). Arts of the Contact Zone. *Profession 91*: 33–40.

Smith, Linda Tuhiwai (2012). *Decolonizing Methodologies: Research and Indigenous Peoples*. Second Edition. London and New York: Zed Books.

Spade, D (2013). Intersectional Resistance and Law Reform. *Signs 38*(4): 1031–1055.

Steele, C.M. (1997). A Threat in the Air: How Stereotypes Shape Intellectual Identity and Performance. *American Psychologist 52*(6): 613.

Tuck, E. (2009). Suspending Damage: A Letter to Communities. *Harvard Educational Review 79*(3): 409–428.

Tuck, E., and M. McKenzie (2014). *Place in Research: Theory, Methodology, and Methods.* New York: Routledge.

Wynter, S. (2003). Unsettling the Coloniality of Being/Power/Truth/Freedom: Towards the Human, after Man, Its Overrepresentation – an Argument. *Centennial Review 3*(3): 257–337.

INDEX

Taylor & Francis eBooks

Helping you to choose the right eBooks for your Library

Add Routledge titles to your library's digital collection today. Taylor and Francis ebooks contains over 50,000 titles in the Humanities, Social Sciences, Behavioural Sciences, Built Environment and Law.

Choose from a range of subject packages or create your own!

Benefits for you

» Free MARC records
» COUNTER-compliant usage statistics
» Flexible purchase and pricing options
» All titles DRM-free.

Benefits for your user

» Off-site, anytime access via Athens or referring URL
» Print or copy pages or chapters
» Full content search
» Bookmark, highlight and annotate text
» Access to thousands of pages of quality research at the click of a button.

REQUEST YOUR **FREE** INSTITUTIONAL TRIAL TODAY	**Free Trials Available** We offer free trials to qualifying academic, corporate and government customers.

eCollections – Choose from over 30 subject eCollections, including:

Archaeology	Language Learning
Architecture	Law
Asian Studies	Literature
Business & Management	Media & Communication
Classical Studies	Middle East Studies
Construction	Music
Creative & Media Arts	Philosophy
Criminology & Criminal Justice	Planning
Economics	Politics
Education	Psychology & Mental Health
Energy	Religion
Engineering	Security
English Language & Linguistics	Social Work
Environment & Sustainability	Sociology
Geography	Sport
Health Studies	Theatre & Performance
History	Tourism, Hospitality & Events

For more information, pricing enquiries or to order a free trial, please contact your local sales team: www.tandfebooks.com/page/sales

Routledge
Taylor & Francis Group

The home of Routledge books

www.tandfebooks.com